Managers tell.
Leaders listen.

Managers administer.
Leaders innovate.

Managers maintain.
Leaders develop.

Managers rely on systems.
Leaders rely on people.

Managers count on control.
Leaders count on trust.

Manager do things right.
Leaders do the right things.

Managers play "not to lose."
Leaders play to win.

Managers critique.
Leaders coach.

The message is clear! An exciting future awaits those who choose to graduate from traditional management to the elevated ranks of Leadership. Like anything else in life, whether you do or whether you don't is entirely up to you. You truly are the steward of your own destiny.

You are invited to earn your *License to Lead.*

License to Lead

License to Lead

Breakthrough Leadership and Coaching Skills to Accelerate People, Performance and Profits!

by

Ross Buchanan

published with the assistance of

Co-Publishing
a division of Addison Graphics Ltd.

Front Cover Photo: Jonathan Cruz
Back Cover Photo: Ron Sangha

ISBN 0-919869-06-8

Canadian Cataloguing in Publication Data

Buchanan, Ross, 1952-
License to lead

(Self-counsel non-fiction)
ISBN 0-919869-06-8

1. Leadership. 2. Executive ability. I. Title. II. Series.
HD38.2.B82 1995 658.4'092 C95-911035-6

Printing History:

First Printing:	1995
Second Printing:	1996
Expanded Edition	1997

Published with the assistance of
Co-Publishing
a division of Addison Graphics Ltd.

Printed in Canada by Addison Graphics Ltd.

Distribution address:
Strategic Training International
#700 - 555 West Hastings Street
Vancouver, British Columbia
V6B 4N5

Acknowledgments

As you can imagine, a book like this cannot be created by one person alone. I am deeply appreciative of the contributions and encouragement of my clients and friends from whom I have learned so much.

In addition, I thank my wife and partner, Charleen, whose support and belief in me makes my work possible.

Finally, Colleen and Kyle who I am honored to be able to call my children.

What if your people really were your organization's most valuable resource?

And through your ***Leadership and Coaching,*** *you could help them unlock all of the power and potential you know they possess?*

Together, what could you accomplish?

How far could you reach?

License to Lead

Preface to Expanded Edition

Since originally writing the first edition of License To Lead, things could not have gone any better. I am blessed with the opportunity to work with some of the most successful firms and their people from across North America. License To Lead has become a runaway, underground best seller and our Leadership Development Workshops such as Leadership Strategies and Coaching for Commitment continue to win high praise from all of the participants.

I just can't say enough about our clients. Many of the additional ideas incorporated into this expanded edition, of License To Lead are a result of their thoughts and comments. As I have worked with Leaders to help them impact the three P's of business - People, Performance and Profits, I am fortunate that I have been able to learn and benefit from their collective wealth of expertise and experience. To you, my clients, I offer my heartfelt thanks.

In this edition, I have complemented the original text with my ideas on some of the most current Leadership issues of the day. Of the supplemental material added to this expanded edition, I have no doubt that Coaching for Commitment ranks at the top of the list for opportunity and potential. As I continue to work with Leadership Teams, I have come to realize that coaching may very well be the most underdeveloped and underutilized business skill available to managers today.

Our experience of working with clients in our Leadership Strategies Workshops is that managers realize the incredible potential for improved results if they were to coach their people but for the most part, managers have never been given the opportunity to develop strong business coaching skills. If enhancing your ability as a coach is of interest to you, you will be especially interested in the chapter on Coaching for Commitment.

In complementing the original License To Lead with the supplemental material on Coaching for Commitment and other issues such as The Practices of Exemplary Leaders and The Language of Success, I have added to the page count and the amount of time required to read this book and complete the exercises. One of the primary purposes of License To Lead is to serve as a preparation guide for our corporate clients participating in our Leadership Strategies Workshops. As such, I strive to be as concise and clear as possible in communicating what others would often like you to think are complex and sophisticated concepts. The reality is that much of Leadership is based on common sense.

Abe Lincoln is reported to have said, "It takes a couple of weeks to write a good twenty minute speech; but I can talk for two or three hours with no preparation at all." Much of the same is true of my writing of this book.

Rather than add complexity to the issues of Leadership, one of my goals in writing License To Lead has always been to avoid complicating the topic. I seek to be as clear and concise as possible.

Personally, I will not be happy until I am able to synthesize the primary principles of Leadership down to a 10-page brochure. If you are currently in a Leadership role, actively managing a portion of a business, leading a life outside of business, and preparing to participate in one of our Leadership Development programs, you know exactly what I mean. The concise and calculated format of License To Lead is a deliberate strategy to make it as reader friendly as possible. With the limited time available to you, I encourage you to spend your time wisely and familiarize yourself with the concepts in this book.

This book is not intended to be academic, complex, touchy-feely, nor a quick fix. But rather, License To Lead is deeply rooted in common sense. The kind of common sense that is rarely practiced, but when it is, produces impressive results for all concerned. My experience has been that what is common sense is seldom common practice. When it comes to Leadership and Coaching the answers, "the real answers," are not in this book. The answers are within you. You already know!

In writing License to Lead and developing our Leadership Development Workshops, I hope to provide you with a springboard to convert that which you already know into action. Knowing it doesn't matter. It is only doing it that really makes the difference. With Leadership and Coaching, as with so many other things in life, we need to stop intellectualizing and start actualizing.

I have come to realize that what separates the Leaders from the dreamers is courage and commitment. Courage to take the first step and the commitment to keep going. Yes, Leadership is an action word.

I hope to see you at the workshops!

Ross Buchanan

"The mother of all Leadership errors is that Leaders think the purpose of their people is to serve them, rather than the other way around."

Ross Buchanan

Introduction

As I work with businesses across North America in a Consulting capacity, I have identified what I believe to be an incredible opportunity to improve results. My experience has been that the #1 element that sets successful firms apart from average or struggling companies is Leadership.

You will be interested to know that my own empirical research clearly shows that struggling and average companies are often populated by good people but are desperately lacking Leadership. Good people - no Leadership! If there is a Leadership presence, it all rests on one person and is not dispersed and multiplied throughout the Management Team.

It is for this reason that I have focused my resources to the task of helping my clients develop the "Leadership Effectiveness" of all of the members of their Management Team. Make no mistake about it, everything in your organization rises and falls on Leadership.

Research clearly shows that 60% of the North American work force said that they could "double" their contribution to their employers if there was "more in it for them." And what does "more in it for them" really mean? As managers, we typically interpret this statement to mean more money. But in fact, we couldn't be more wrong.

The top three things that people are looking for from their managers are:

1. Inclusion
2. Appreciation
3. Accountability

Inclusion rather than exclusion. Appreciation rather than being taken for granted. Accountability - the accountability of themselves and their associates to perform to expectations.

So why is it that so many managers fail so miserably at Leadership? I think that much of the answer lies with the fact that the skills that accelerated their promotion to management are very different from the skills that they require to graduate to the next logical level of success - Leadership. Management is appointed - Leadership is earned. When you think of it, most people who move to management are very independent, task oriented people. Yet when you look at effective Leadership, you see how independence and unbalanced task orientation can be major drawbacks in achieving your Leadership mission of "helping your people become the best that they possibly can be." There is no doubt in my mind that to succeed as an effective Leader today, you need to graduate from independence to interdependence.

Interdependence is the ability to work together, co-operatively to help those around you to multiply their success. The poor qualities of an ineffective Leader are often those of a Manager caught in the trap of independence. Descriptions such as "won't let go," "does not trust us," "will not listen," "keeps us in the dark," "doesn't care about us," are all typical descriptions of an independently oriented manager. Switching from independence to interdependence is an excellent opportunity to continue to grow and develop the skills and strategies that the most successful Leaders utilize to help their people achieve exciting results.

Effective Leadership can be learned. Effective Leadership is about Vision, Attitude, Shared Expectations, Accountability, Inclusion, Priorities, Appreciation, Communication, Change, Focus, Coaching, Empowerment, Synergy, Creativity, Delegation, and most importantly, about how all of these pieces of the Leadership puzzle fit together to impact people. These are all "learned" skills. And while not everyone will be a great Leader, we can all be better Leaders. It is not easy to acquire the skills of effective Leadership but the rewards of doing so are beyond description.

There was a time not that long ago that the people who had the responsibility in a company, branch, or department sat in their offices and managed what they could. That is exactly what they were expected to do - manage. For the most part, they tried to deal with whatever problems presented themselves, and then called it a day.

Back when the business world was a much simpler place, management like this was fine thank you. Rarely visionary, but fine as long as life rolled predictably along.

Welcome to today's reality! Mere management simply is not enough anymore. This world is too unpredictable, too volatile, and too fast moving for such an uninspired approach. What is needed now is something much deeper - Leadership; to help people achieve what they are truly capable of, to establish a vision for the future, to encourage, to coach, to mentor, and to build and maintain successful relationships.

In the words of Harvard professor John Quelch, "Back when business operated in a more stable environment, management skills were sufficient. But when the business environment becomes volatile, when the waters are uncharted, when your mission requires a greater flexibility than you ever imagined it would - that is when Leadership skills are critical."

The Inverted Triangle

As part of my research for this book I sought out the opinions of many. One of the questions I asked is, "What do you think is the number one mistake that most Leaders make?" One response was more frequent than all the others. Most people felt that the error commonly committed by Leaders was to think that their employees were there to serve them rather than the other way around.

Traditional organizations have been structured based on the triangle with the Leader at the top and the base of the organization spreading out below. The obvious implication being that all things good in life flow from the top down. This kind of arrogance results in an autocratic, domineering style of ineffective Leadership. Not only does this quasi-militaristic approach not work now, but guaranteed, it will not work in the future. I call this the "Superiority" style of Leadership. Some of the symptoms that you might expect to see from this poor Leadership style include:

An abuse of authority,

Very little listening and even less hearing,

Control characterized by an unwillingness to let go,

Poor delegation,

Big egos,

Inadequate sharing of information,

Lack of openness,

And it's contagious. I have seen it time and time again. The president barks at the vice-president, so the V.P. barks at the department heads, who in turn bark at the employees. Pretty soon, with all of this barking, it is starting to sound like a kennel. And what happens when the employees start barking at the customers? Oh well, we just can't imagine how that could have happened.

One of the most damaging implications of the top down, Superiority style of Leadership is that all of the people are focused internally. They are distracted by what the Leader wants, and in turn their overall effectiveness is diluted. By converting to a bottom up, "Supportive" style of Leadership, your people will be able to focus externally on their clients and the opportunities. In doing so they will be free to positively contribute to the overall success of the organization. I call this the **evolution of the inverted triangle.**

My experience has been that the top down, Superiority style of Leadership is very common and it comes to us quite easily. Many of us are conditioned to develop this style. Many of the models that we may have been exposed to, as we climbed the corporate ladder, reflected this type of Leadership. In fact, the bottom up, Supportive style of Leadership, is quite rare but without a doubt, is practiced by the most successful Leaders that I have had an opportunity to work with. Those that are producing the most exciting results see themselves clearly at the bottom of an inverted triangle. At the bottom of the inverted triangle practicing the "Helping Habit." They are helping their people to succeed.

Which style of Leadership do you practice, Superiority

or Supportive? Have you inverted the triangle in your organization, your department, or your branch yet? The top down, Superiority style of Leadership is characterized by the person who thinks that everyone in their organization should serve them, as opposed to them serving everyone in the organization.

Superiority style Leaders have a tendency to focus on the hard issues and to do whatever they can to avoid the soft issues. They have developed a strong problem orientation. They think their lot in life is to find problems and fix them. Much of their time is spent in a reactive mode of fighting fires.

On the other hand the Supportive style Leaders tend to be sensitive to both the hard and soft issues, and in doing so are more oriented to solutions and opportunities rather than problems.

The following charts will help you identify your current style of Leadership.

Superiority Leader

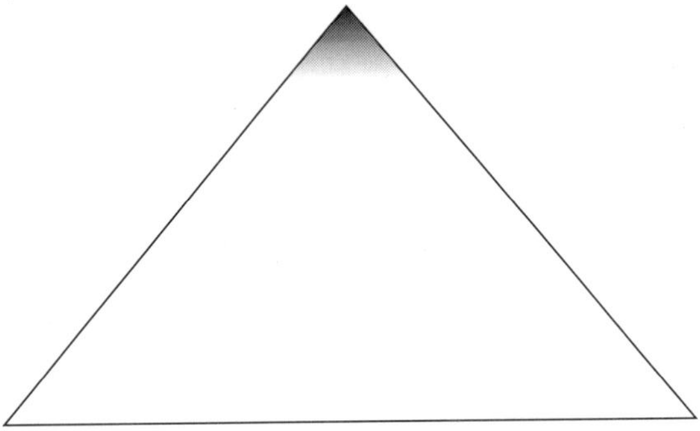

Characteristics and attributes of a Leader practicing the Superiority Style are that they:

are definitely tellers;

feel a need to personally make all of the decisions;

have strong opinions of everyone and everything;

condition employees to wait for and expect direction;

are running scared of losing control;

are consumed by problems, problems, problems;

can be very moody;

analyze every little thing to death;

are addicted to meetings;

are very task oriented and consistently push for results;

believe that they need to have all of the answers;

have to be right all of the time.

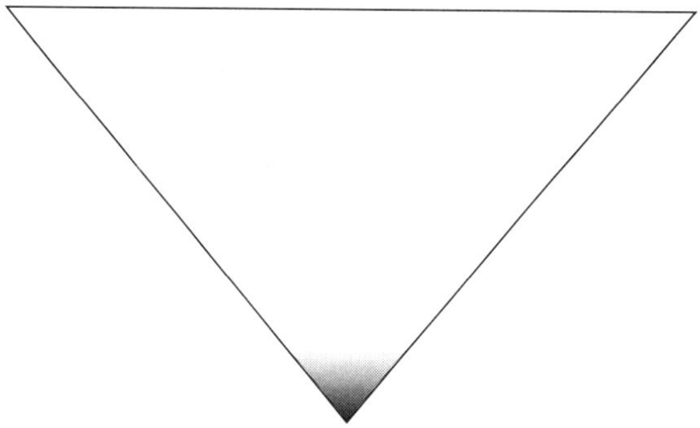

Supportive Leader

Characteristics and attributes of a Leader practicing the Supportive or Helping style are that they:

are seen by others as an asker;

empower people;

are open minded and receptive to new ideas;

reinforce personal responsibility among their team;

set the people free to produce results;

focus on solutions and opportunities;

are not subject to wild mood swings;

listen to their own heart;

empower people to do their own thing;

focus on the vision;

have lost their inflated ego;

know that they can err and allow others to do the same.

The shift in attitude towards a powerful, fully empowered organization must start at the top of the organization. And the first step is for the top to move to the bottom!

The Ivory Tower Syndrome

Typically the Leader is seen as the person at the top of the heap. The person who has "made it." Leaders are perceived as self-assured and in control of their own destiny. Let me assure you that nothing is further from the truth. There can be a no more lonely and isolated place than that of executive Leadership in corporate America today. Quite frankly, many of the Leaders that I meet with are just plain scared and lonely. And is it any wonder when you consider the magnitude of the responsibility that they feel? Combine this with the high degree of visibility that many of them are exposed to, certainly within their organization, perhaps in their industry, sometimes on a even grander stage and you will start to understand why they feel the way that they do.

Gone are the days that executive Leadership meant a job for as long as you wanted it. The shareholders of today are looking for results and they are looking for results now. In the new reality of business, if the team is not performing it is not the players that are fired, but rather the coach.

One of the most significant problems for many executive Leaders to overcome is what I call the Ivory Tower Syndrome. What I am really talking about is executive Leaders being removed and isolated from the reality of what is happening on the front lines and in the trenches. Independent Leaders who surround themselves with dependent managers magnify the problem even more. They are reliant on people who are likely to tell the Leader what they think they want to hear, rather than what is really happening.

To be certain that you avoid this trap of isolation, it is important that you work to communicate with all levels and areas within your organization. Some of the most effective ways to maintain good communication with your people are to walk around your operations, hold advisory groups, conduct employee surveys, and of course, use the good old suggestion box. In order to keep in touch with your customers, there is no better method than to get out of your office and visit your customers face to face.

This strategy of meeting with your customers face to face achieves a number of positive results. First of all, it sends a message to the customers that they are so important that you, as the Leader, are personally visiting them. Secondly, it gives you an excellent opportunity to learn first hand what your customers are thinking and what they may be looking for in the future. Thirdly it sends a real message to your entire organization about the importance of the customer. Finally, it will be seen as being very supportive by the members of your organization.

With all of these benefits in mind you have to wonder why any Leaders are sitting in their offices. The answer is that they are probably managing rather than Leading. Nothing gives me greater pleasure than to phone one of my clients only to be told that they are unavailable because they are out of the office meeting with customers. That's great! Why is it that my more successful clients seem to be out visiting customers and the less successful clients are often available to immediately take my calls? The kind of actions we are talking about to escape the Ivory Tower Syndrome requires proactive steps. Sure it feels safe and comfortable to reside in our offices and function in a reactive state. But how safe and comfortable is it really? How long can you exist in this reactive mode?

As a Leader, you have the responsibility for making the final decision. You will never get all of the credit when things are going well, but guaranteed you will be under the spotlight when things start to go sour. With this kind of exposure in mind, it is important that you have a total and clear picture of the situation before making an informed decision. In order to assure the totality and clarity of your information, it is important to ensure that you are getting your information from a wide variety of sources. Your best source of information? Those people who are actively involved on the front lines. In all of my experience with helping our clients develop the Leadership effectiveness of their people, the very best solutions, the ones that repeatedly produce the greatest degree of success, come from those people who are actively involved with the issues on a day to day basis. By choosing to include those involved with the issue in the decision making process, you are guaranteed a happier, more committed team of people. The great news is that within your organization are some of the best experts in their field – your very own people.

The Charismatic Leader

Early in my career, I was easily impressed by what I would call a charismatic style of Leadership. But now that I have had an opportunity to study Leaders in action, and to take a look at the kind of results that they help their people achieve, I understand that charismatic Leadership is both limited and limiting. It is limited in the significant contribution that it can really make to an organization, and very limiting to the other members of the firm.

Researchers have identified four common problems that often surface where charismatic Leadership is involved:

1. Charismatic Leaders set unrealistic expectations both within their organization and with their customers.

2. Charismatic Leaders create an organizational dependency that has everyone sitting in neutral, parked on the sidelines, waiting for the next directive from the boss.

3. The lower levels of management become meaningless because charismatic Leaders become so big in everyone's minds, that unless the vision, reward, suggestion, guidance, or criticism comes from them, it does not have any credibility.

4. Charismatic Leaders create a need for continuing magic which often leaves everyone in the organization sitting around waiting for the magic show. The charismatic Leader has been able to pull the rabbit out of the hat before, so why not this time.

Well sooner or later, no matter how charismatic the Leader may be they just run out of rabbits or move the show elsewhere, leaving a highly dependent organization wondering what happened.

Action Plan ... Converting Ideas Into Action

1. Review the characteristics and attributes of a Supportive Leader. Based on a scale of 0 to 10 how do you think your people would rate you?

2. If there was one or two areas that would hold the greatest opportunity for your improvement, what might they be?

3. What steps could you take to improve in these areas?

4. If you were able to successfully improve in these areas and develop a more effective Supportive Style of Leadership, what kind of impact might it have on you personally and professionally? What kind of impact might it have on your people?

Focus, Focus, Focus

I just can't overemphasize the importance of Focus as a critical Leadership principle. After all, what is Leadership all about if it is not marshaling our limited resources and focusing our efforts to maximize our results? In today's economy, with all of the exciting opportunities that we are consistently introduced to, it is so easy to be distracted from the optimum target. Distractions lead to diluted results.

As I work with clients, I consistently see a lack of focus as one of the critical factors that separates the successful organizations from those that experience average or struggling performance.

This factor is becoming even more important as many organizations are becoming "leaner and meaner." With fewer people being asked to do more, it is so important that each person's efforts be properly focused. They should be focused in a direction that supports and complements the organization's overall vision of the future.

There is no doubt in my mind that the most successful Leaders are absolutely ruthless about focusing the allocation of their resources. By channeling their scattered resources into a focused beam of energy, they are able to achieve exciting results.

One of the key ingredients of Focus is the need for a pro-active Leader. This is one of the considerations that I believe differentiates Leadership from management. I see Leaders pro-actively creating a vision of the future, and focusing their resources to achieve their goals. On the other hand, I see traditional management in a much different mindset. I see traditional managers as being reactive to situations rather than pro-actively creating their future. Every person has the choice to take action rather than being acted upon.

The 80/20 Rule, or Pareto Principle, certainly has validity when you are discussing Leadership. You just can't over-estimate the unimportance of practically everything. In fact, if you are trapped in a traditional management mind-set, you are probably focused on activity and treat everything as important. Successful Leaders are very good at letting go of the unimportant and, in doing so, focusing their talent and energies on those areas that will produce the most significant results. When working with clients who I sense are struggling with activity, rather than results which produce success, I encourage them to identify their handful of "High Return Activities," the activities that will help them produce the most desirable results. Once these High Return Activities are identified, I then encourage my clients to create a reminder for themselves. A "bull's eye" identifying those High Return Activities enables them to stay focused and to avoid having their efforts diluted by the multitude of potential distractions. Focus! Focus! Focus!

Action Plan ... Converting Ideas Into Action

1. As a Leader, what are the "High Return Activities" that you should be focusing on?

2. If you were able to give these "High Return Activities" the attention that they deserve, what kind of impact would they have on the success of your organization and your effectiveness as a Leader?

3. What could you do to be able to better focus on your "High Return Activities?"

"Coming together is a beginning. Keeping together is progress. Working together is success."

Henry Ford

High Performance Environment

How important a factor do you think a person's work environment is to their success? Let me ask the question another way. Do you think that a person in a "Low Performance Environment" could really achieve exciting results? Of course not! Yet why is it that so little attention is given to the issue of creating a "High Performance Environment?"

When I speak of a "High Performance Environment" I am referring to an environment that naturally brings out the best in people and allows them to "bloom and blossom." How does one achieve this lofty goal? By simply supporting the things that are important to the lives of your people. Who knows what they really want their work environment to be like? Of course–your people do.

Our experience of working with clients has been that by providing a workplace, that is in alignment with what your people want, creates a happy, energized environment. One thing is for certain, if your workplace is not "in alignment" with your people then it is "out of alignment," and carries all of the negative connotations that this implies.

Some of the critical factors that people typically tell us they want in their work environments include:

- clear, concise goals
- appreciation
- a strong, co-operative, team mindset
- inclusion
- an opportunity to take responsibility
- trust
- a clean, comfortable environment
- a vision of the future
- a winning attitude
- recognition of the value of the people
- commitment to continuous growth and development of the people
- good communications
- freedom
- commitment to high quality
- seen as an industry Leader
- competitive compensation
- challenging work opportunities
- responsive Leadership
- good resources
- "open minded" colleagues
- a fun place
- a high degree of professionalism
- freedom to fail

It is important to note that there is only one vision of a High Performance Environment that should really matter to you. That is the vision of your people. Rather than implementing what has worked for others, it is critical to seek the input from all of the participants — Inclusion rather than Exclusion. Inclusion results in a strong sense of commitment.

If the development of a High Performance Environment sounds like a priority to you, my recommendation would be that you get started by gathering your people together and giving them the opportunity to "brainstorm" about what is really important to them. You can see from my examples that none of these factors are really costly to deliver, but they do require a commitment to listen to your people and respond to their wishes.

Blinded by Your Budget

As I work with sales organizations, one error that I often see repeated is what one of my clients calls being "blinded by your budget."

My investigation in this area began when a client's manager explained to me that his department was at 80% of budget. This was presented to me as good news just like a student who scores 80% on an exam would achieve an A on their report card. What this manager saw as good news, I saw as poor performance. Being at 80% to me meant that the department was 20% behind the minimum level targeted for their area.

Make no mistake about it. Leaders set budgets as minimum acceptable targets but far too many people see budgets as Utopia.

With all of the opportunities that exist today we see many of our clients achieving quantum increases in performance. Numbers like 150% and 200% of budget are not unheard of today. Do not let your budgets get in your way. Do not be "blinded by your budget."

Change ... Growth Or Grief?

Not only are we seeing more change today then ever before, but we are seeing it arrive and depart at an ever accelerating rate. Will the future bring less change? Of course not. Will the pace of change slow down? Not likely!

Many people tell me that they feel as if their world is being turned upside down and inside out. These chaotic times create exciting opportunities for effective Leaders. These are Leaders who have recognized the new reality, one in which the only real constant is change itself.

Can you successfully challenge change? No! To stand up to change, to confront change, or to ignore change, can only produce one result. You will be flattened by the steam roller of change.

In order to successfully operate any organization today calls for a special brand of Leadership. One that recognizes that in today's fast moving markets, business needs to be practiced very differently than in the past. Whatever it was that you did to get you here just isn't good enough to even keep you where you are, let alone get you where you need to be.

Never before has there been a more opportune time to practice the Japanese business philosophy of Kaizen.

Kaizen is all about continuous improvement, the need to be constantly on the lookout for new and better ways to accomplish things through gradual, unending improvement.

Those firms that will continue to thrive in the future will be those that are populated by Leaders who are open-minded and receptive to change. Successful Leaders need to be able to adapt to the new realities and change at least as quickly as the industries and markets that they function in.

In his book, "Leadership Is An Art," Max Depree tells us that "In the end, it is important to remember that we cannot become what we need to be by remaining what we are." In the new reality of today's business climate the fact is that if you stop changing, you are dead in the water.

A belief that I strongly hold is that absolutely everything in an organization rises and falls on the Leadership effectiveness of its key people. How critical a role do Leaders play in creating a change friendly attitude within their firm? Absolute. People do exactly what people see and if the Leader is resistant to change, is it any wonder that the followers also resist.

As I have worked with Leaders, I have developed a short list of what I call The Characteristics and Attributes of Ineffective Leadership. Based on my experience ineffective Leaders:

1. Do not understand people
2. Are not very imaginative
3. Seldom take responsibility
4. Are not very well organized
5. Often are plagued by problems of a personal nature
6. Are "fat and happy" with their achievements

7. Are resistant to risk

8. Fight change

9. Lack a sense of team spirit

10. Are quick to show anger and rage

It is interesting to note that a full 50% of these characteristics and attributes are directly related to an inability or unwillingness to change. Effective Leadership today calls for the ultimate skills of an agent of change. And yes this can be a very scary assignment. In the words of Machiavelli, "There is nothing more difficult to take in hand, more perilous to conduct, or more uncertain in its success, than to take the lead in the introduction of a new order of things."

Where should we start to deal with change? Leadership really is an inside job. The only logical place to start is with yourself. In your role of a Leader it is absolutely critical that you lead by example. It is only once that you have changed yourself that you qualify for the opportunity to change others.

> *"I was a revolutionary when I was young and my prayer to God was 'Lord, give me the energy to change the world.' As I approached middle age and realized that my life was half gone without my changing a single soul, I changed my prayer to; 'Lord, give me the grace to change all those who come into contact with me, just my family and friends, and I shall be satisfied.' Now that I am an old man and my days are numbered, I have begun to see how foolish I have been. My one prayer now is; 'Lord, give me the grace to change myself.' If I had prayed for this right from the start, I would not have wasted my life."*
>
> - an unknown Middle Eastern mystic

In order to continue to Lead, you need to continue to change. The sad truth is that far too many executives today who achieve positions of Leadership, become resistant to change and seem intent on desperately attempting to cling to the "good old days." To be an effective Leader you must maintain the attitude of being totally receptive to new ideas. The moment that you lock the gates of change in your mind is the moment that you will cease to be an effective Leader. Once you are through changing, you are through.

I can not overemphasize the importance of Leading by example. Andrew Carnegie said, "As I grow older, I pay less attention to what men say. I just watch what they do." Do you walk the talk? I guarantee your people are watching. In fact the spotlights are on, the sound system turned up, and the tape is rolling.

As a Leader, there is absolutely nothing that is more difficult to undertake, or more uncertain in its success, than change. Resistance to change is an awesome universal power. Is it any wonder why people feel the way that they do? Change is disruptive to our patterns of life and at the same time change creates a high degree of fear of the unknown. These two factors alone are enough to defeat most efforts to change.

My experience has been that people don't resist change as much as they resist being made to change. If people are not included in the decision to change, it is guaranteed they will resist it. It is not the change itself that is the problem but rather the process of implementation. The fact that they are being excluded from the decision making process of change rather than being included is often their primary reason for resistance.

In evaluating change there will always be one question that immediately jumps to the forefront of our minds. "How will this change affect me personally?" In evaluating any potential change it is wise to look at each of the people who will be impacted and to anticipate what their answers to this question might be. Your guesstimate of how they might respond to this critical question will give you some insight not only to how they will respond, but also why they feel the way that they do.

I learned a long time ago that there is a right time and a wrong time for everything, and not only a right time and a wrong time but also a best time. As a strategist, it is critical that each Leader evaluate the timing of each proposed change. "Is now the right time?"

When it comes to timing, the wrong decision at the wrong time, the wrong decision at the right time or the right decision at the wrong time will produce serious trouble. The only successful combination, the one that is guaranteed to produce exciting results, is the right decision at the right time. This magic combination of judgment and timing is the stuff that great Leadership is made of, and the combination that will produce significant results.

In his book, "The Seven Habits of Highly Effective People" the author, Steven Covey, identifies a concept he calls the Emotional Bank Account. Covey uses the Emotional Bank Account as a metaphor to represent the amount of trust that has been built up in a relationship. As we make deposits, we build a wealth of trust. Warren Bennis and Bert Nanus in their book, "Leaders," tell us that "trust is the emotional glue that binds followers and Leaders together." Efforts to produce change without a healthy balance in your Emotional Bank Account will bankrupt your results. Without trust between the Leader and the people, your efforts to change will produce disaster.

One of the keys to successfully implement change is to position it as effectively as possible. Some of the key strategies include timing, the development of allies, leading by example, and focusing on what the proposed changes might mean to those effected. Without the necessary attention being paid to the strategic aspects of orchestrating change, your best ideas could be blindsided by the incredible power of resistance to change. When it comes to change, like many other things in life, properly positioned is half sold.

As I look into the future, I am convinced that a Leader's ability to respond to the challenges of change will have more impact than any other time in history. Without a doubt, only those organizations that are innovative, creative, flexible and adaptable will be able to survive and thrive in the new reality. In order to create a change friendly corporate culture the Leaders of today and tomorrow must continue to remain open minded to new ideas and remain ruthlessly committed to the concept of gradual unending improvement. It is only when your organization is working in alignment with the current realities of your markets that you will be able to ensure a successful future for all concerned. If you do not change, if your organization is out of alignment with the realities of your markets, you and your people will suffer and as a Leader you will fail. You will fail yourself and fail your people.

So does change represent growth or grief? I will let you answer this question for yourself but in my mind there is only one factor that determines whether or not change produces growth or grief. That critical factor is "you."

Remember, "If nothing changes, nothing changes."

Action Plan ... Converting Ideas Into Action

1. Knowing what you know about your industry and your markets, what should your organization be doing now to prepare for what your reality could look like 12 months from now? 36 months from now?

2. What could you personally be doing to prepare better for the future?

3. If you are able to anticipate the future and better position your organization, what might some of the benefits be?

Leaders Are Decisive

Yes, Leaders really are decisive. If you doubt this statement even for a moment, I encourage you to consider the opposite. Leaders are indecisive. Not likely!

Peter Drucker, the author of "Management: Tasks, Responsibilities, and Practices" tells us that "Whenever you see a successful business, someone once made a courageous decision." In fact, somebody has made a series of decisions that have culminated in success. It is these courageous decisions that allow organizations to move forward.

The greatest opponents to these decisions are uncertainty and risk, but the price of indecisiveness is high. Take a look around you in your organization or your industry, and you will start to see the incredible price that we pay for indecisiveness. When things went poorly, where were the Leaders when the decisions had to be made? They were parked in neutral, with the whirlwind of change swirling around them. Not only did their indecisiveness park them in neutral but also left entire organizations on the sidelines. At what cost? The cost of millions of dollars of lost opportunities. The cost of laying people off their jobs. The cost of entire organizations that have been sabotaged because no Leaders stepped forward to make the hard decisions when they needed to be made.

I see it week after week — indecisiveness. Multi-million dollar organizations investing countless hours of management's time over a period of months to arrive at a decision on something like whether or not to buy some desks, or what color the carpeting in the lunch room should be. While their brain cells are being consumed on these kinds of issues, what is happening to the real decisions that need to be made about their business, their clients, and their future?

Decisions need to be made by those who have the greatest vested interest in the outcome. That is where

Leadership has to step in and make the best decisions. The best decisions for all concerned in a reasonable time frame.

Don't get me wrong. I strongly believe in all of the good things that we have already said about teams and inclusion, but at the end of the day if an organization is to retain a sense of direction, Leadership needs to act and make the best decisions. In North America today I see so many organizations searching for the perfect solution. A perfect solution that seldom exists, rather than the best solution. In doing so, the indecisiveness that results leaves the organization wandering aimlessly without a clear path. Sure everyone seems busy. They are running here and running there, but what are they really accomplishing?

Decisive Leaders provide organizations with the direction that they require to succeed. To ignore this responsibility of Leadership is a guaranteed formula for decay and rot.

In order to move forward in today's competitive environment, not only to just survive but to thrive, Leadership needs to take a more decisive stance. Stop deliberating and start deciding! The cost of not doing so is just too high.

Anybody can sit on a beach or soak in a hot tub and deliberate. As a Leader your responsibility to your organization and your people is to get off the beach or out of the hot tub and make a decision to take action.

A Short Story

Three frogs are sitting on a log. Two of the frogs decide to jump into the pond. How many frogs are left on the log?

Three! The two frogs only decided to jump into the pond, they didn't actually jump. Jump in. Make a splash. Get wet and swim like crazy.

Action Plan ... Converting Ideas Into Action

1. What decisions are you currently considering that have consumed too much time relative to their potential impact?

2. For each of these situations, what would be the best decision, and when will you act on it?

3. How would your colleagues rate your decisiveness (0 - 10)?

4. If you were to adopt a more decisive Leadership role, what might some of the benefits be?

Hardening of the Attitudes

Without a doubt, your people are the lifeblood of your organization. If it weren't for the energy and intellect of your people, your organization would have died a long time ago.

Just as humans abuse their bodies so do organizations abuse their people. In the same manner that poor nutrition, bad habits, and lack of exercise leads to a build up of plaque on the walls of the heart's arteries, our ineffective habits of management serve to narrow the diameter of our organizational arteries reducing the free flow of creative contributions from our people. What happens when the diameter of an artery is narrowed, reducing the flow of blood in the human body? You are absolutely right! The big one....a Heart Attack!

This is exactly what happens to organizations as a result of bad management habits such as exclusion or lack of appreciation. It gradually deteriorates the health of your organization, narrowing the walls of your organizational arteries and one day, it happens....Kabooooom!

While poor management habits can kill an organization just as poor health habits kill people, the good news is that we can do something about it. As humans we have the choice to practice good health habits and the same kind of choices are available to the Leaders of organizations. The personal choice to practice habits of effective Leadership that will ensure a healthy, thriving organization.

Let me ask you this? How important a role do you think a Leader's attitude plays in determining his or her level of success? If you are like the hundreds of people I have asked this question, your answer will be that attitude plays a major role in determining a Leader's ability. In fact, my own empirical research concludes that if there is one factor that differentiates successful Leaders from those who struggle, it may very well be attitude.

How is your attitude? If you have a great attitude, congratulations. I encourage you to cherish it and grow it. Treat it as if it is your most important asset. Life is not so much what happens to us, but rather how we react to what we experience. Our reactions are governed by our attitudes. And who is responsible for our attitudes? You are absolutely right! As individuals, we are each personally responsible for our own attitudes.

We are already sensitive to how a Leader can leverage his or her talents throughout their organization, and in doing so, multiply the overall success of the entire organization. The same kind of leveraged opportunity exists for attitudes, both good attitudes as well as bad attitudes. Without a doubt the Leader's attitude will impact the attitudes of his or her people. I believe that a Leader's attitude will often become contagious throughout the entire organization. It is for this reason that Leaders, who are committed to Leading by example, take the time to audit their own attitudes, and if necessary, make the required adjustments.

Personally, I know that one of my weaknesses is to take myself too seriously. Whenever I find myself in this trap, I will make a point of picking up the phone or getting face to face with one of my clients who has a healthy attitude. I know that all I need to make the necessary adjustments is to spend a few moments talking with one of these Leaders. Their attitudes really are contagious.

From time to time I experience Leaders who are suffering from what I call "Hardening of the Attitudes." Some of the most noticeable symptoms of this deadly disease include:

1. Taking oneself too seriously.

2. Starting to believe that the purpose of your people is to serve you rather than the other way around.

3. Thinking that you are the only one in the organization that is capable of making the best decisions.

4. Not valuing the ideas of your people on the front lines.

If you sense that you may have been exposed to this disease, let me recommend that you take immediate action. Not only is it important that we develop healthy attitudes in "the gardens of our minds" but it is equally important that we weed our garden to dispose of unhealthy attitudes just like we would hoe the weeds in our garden so that they do not start to starve out the healthy plants.

Far too often I see organizations launch significant efforts at change such as restructuring the business or releasing key people when all they really needed was to change their attitudes. We can experience the most radical, most significant changes in our lives by simply changing our attitudes.

The philosopher William James probably said it best

when he said, "The greatest discovery of my generation is that a human being can alter his life by altering his attitude."

Take a moment and write down the names of a few people you know that you hold a high degree of respect for. Now, beside each of these people write down what it is that you like about them the most. Based on my experience, the odds are very high that what you wrote down had everything in the world to do with attitude. What does that tell you?

Positive attitudes are a choice. They are a choice that I encourage you, as a Leader, to make and renew each and every day of your life. In the words of Hugh Downs, "A happy person is not a person in a certain set of circumstances, but rather a person with a certain set of attitudes."

Enthusiasm

No discussion about the impact of attitudes would be complete without acknowledging the importance of enthusiasm.

Ralph Waldo Emerson once described enthusiasm this way. "Every great and commanding movement is the triumph of enthusiasm. Nothing great was ever achieved without it."

Enthusiasm is a special feeling. It does not necessarily mean jumping up and down, doing cartwheels, or talking loud. Some of the most powerful enthusiasm can be as simple as a twinkle in an eye or a chuckle in a voice. One of my clients, a Leader who naturally emotes great enthusiasm tells me that it is something that can never be taken for granted in an organization. He believes that enthusiasm is something that needs to be constantly given the attention it deserves. He should know. You can see his naturally enthusiastic manner spread to, and positively impact, those around him.

I can guarantee that, as a Leader, your people will never be more enthusiastic about something than you are. When it comes to the level of enthusiasm in your organization, you really do set the pace.

Action Plan ... Converting Ideas Into Action

1. What words do you think others would use to describe your attitude?

2. What words would you like others to think of when they describe your attitude?

3. What kind of changes should you, and could you make to improve your attitude?

Your Most Valuable Resource — People

As you work within your specific industries, whether you are a manufacturer of tractors, a distributor of electronics, or a government services organization, it is so easy to forget that we are all really in the same business. The people business.

Your people are your organization's most critical resource. No matter what kind of organization you are involved in, absolutely nothing happens until somebody makes it happen.

Take a moment to think about this. The largest single cost in most organizations today is people. Our successes and failures are in the hands of our people. Most of our problems are about people. Most of our time is spent discussing people. In fact as much as 90% of a Leader's time can be invested with people. Are you starting to see what I mean about being in the people business?

When it comes to the topic of people development I find that I have been able to produce the most significant and the most lasting results by focusing on four primary principles:

1. Inclusion

Whenever possible, an effort must be made to include your people in as many parts of your process as possible. Time and time again people tell me that they place a very high value on inclusion. If the people are telling us that inclusion is that important, then you can imagine how they feel when they experience the opposite. Exclusion!

2. Time

Your people require your time. I mean your direct, in the face, eye to eye, ear to ear kind of time. Time that is so important that it is preciously guarded and protected. Do you schedule specific meeting times with your people on a regular basis? If people are really as important as I hear managers tell me they are, why are we not giving them the respect that they deserve. Sure we will gladly schedule a meeting to discuss the "hard" issues such as the mounting investment in Inventory, or how we allowed our Accounts Receivable to get out of hand, but will we place the same kind of priority on the "soft" issues? The funny thing about it is that the so called "soft" issues really are the hardest, in terms of being the most difficult to address. At the same time it is the "soft" things that produce the "hard" results.

In situations where I am facilitating workshops with a client's front line staff, I am often amazed by two things. Early on in the workshops, I ask each of the participants to talk a little about what they are hoping to achieve in the workshops, and to tell us about what life outside of their work looks like. It is in this setting that people will tell you about their real priorities in life. Whether its taking the twins to swimming practice at 5 A.M. every morning, six days a week, or their national success as an amateur golfer, or the fact that they recently completed a College degree after years of night school courses, this is where you discover the real people.

Once we have gone around the room and everyone has had an opportunity to share, I will often call for a quick 5 minute break, and what happens? You would be amazed at how many people get up walk over to one of their associates and express amazement at what they just heard. "John, I didn't know you played in a band. You know I've just taken up the banjo again after being away from it for fifteen years."

If people who work together have to come to my workshops to learn a little about each other, what does that tell you about the interest that we really take in each other at work? Now I am not suggesting that a Leader should become a Social Director, but I am suggesting that if you acknowledge that people really are your most valuable asset, then we better start treating them like it. A great place to start is by committing the time to them that they deserve.

As a Leader, people are not an interruption. Your people are your reason for being.

The other thing that usually happens after a few hours of front-line people working together in a workshop, is for a member of the Management Team to comment that "I am really surprised with you people. This is great stuff you are coming up with."

What is the real message? "You are 40 years old and have been with us for the last 15 or 20 years and it is only now that I am realizing that you aren't a moron."

Time and time again, I am overwhelmed with the

talent and potential of employees, and time and time again, I am amazed at management's inability to recognize and utilize that latent talent.

3. Individuality

Each and every employee is unique and must be treated as an individual. In the rush of day to day crisis management, it is easy to dehumanize the workplace and treat people as a collection of bodies, but without a doubt the most effective Leaders employ a much different strategy. The most successful Leaders make a point of humanizing the workplace by remembering as many names of people as possible. They don't just memorize names but they take a sincere interest in who the people really are and what their interests and contributions are. Your people are people first, second and always. The minute you start to treat them any differently, you can be guaranteed that they will sense it and in doing so become valuable additions to competitive firms that may be able to attract their attention. Your people really are volunteers. In exchange for a biweekly pay check they are volunteering their services. Don't forget that as volunteers they can very easily be attracted to others who take an interest in them as unique individuals.

4. Appreciation

Another trait that I have found to be highly effective in my role as a people developer is to apply appropriate doses of appreciation, recognition and celebration. As a Leader it is vital that you help your people to celebrate their successes. Your people are doing a lot of things right that enables your organization to achieve the kind of success that it does. Let's be certain that we let all of our people know how much we appreciate their efforts.

Any managers who are taking their people for granted these days are simply creating a ton of headaches for themselves. This is so simple I am almost embarrassed by the number of times that I need to repeat it, but your people need constant, healthy doses of appreciation, recognition and celebration. Lets get excited about all of the good things that we are accomplishing!

In a discussion recently, a Historian asked me about what I was working on and I told him of the work I was doing in the field of Leadership Development. He pointed out to me some interesting points on Leadership from a historical perspective that do a good job of reinforcing the role of Leaders as people developers.

I am told that the great Leader, Napoleon knew the name of every officer in his army. Not only did he know all of their names but he was able to recall other key information such as their home town, their past victories in battle, their wives' names and often the names of their children. Is it any wonder that a Leader who took that kind of interest in his people was able to develop such a devoted, loyal army?

Hiring the Right People

I will never forget the client who told me the inside secret to great hiring. "Great Firing!" Let me explain.

As I visited this client's office on a regular basis I could not help but be impressed with the quality of his very professional staff. Picture this. An office staff of close to thirty people all working together in a very impressive manner. I asked the client what is the secret to developing such a great team of people. What is the secret to great hiring?

In responding to my question with the comment "Great Firing" he went on to explain that in the selection process you can only do your best. You can analyze the tests, study the resumes, conduct a series of in-depth interviews , check the references, solicit the opinions of your associates, but there is never any guarantee that your new hire is going to work out for you. Unfortunately, what most organizations do is once they invite a person to join their organization they never let them go, even when they realize that things just aren't working out. Typically after a month or so we know that John isn't right for the job or the job isn't right for John but what do we do? We continue to ignore the situation. Five, ten years down the road, John is still there and he still isn't contributing the way that he should be.

Think of all the brain cells we could have saved and all the frustration that could of been avoided if once we realized a mismatch, we took appropriate action. For the most part, when you realize early on that a person isn't working out, that person is way ahead of you and knows that it isn't working. If you don't take the initiative, the person is unlikely to take the necessary steps to escape the mismatched job. Often when clients recognize a mismatch and suggest to the new employee that it just isn't working out, the employee responds with a sigh of relief and appreciates being set free. In fact, some of my clients who experienced this situation have actually had former employees return some time later and thank the Leader for giving them the nudge they needed to move on and seek more appropriate employment.

Remember, it is not the people you fire that cause you problems. It is the people who you don't fire, but should.

Another trap that I see smaller organizations make is to

compromise on the quality of the person that they are inviting to join their organization. I firmly believe that the smaller the organization the more important it is to search out the ideal new hire. Larger organizations find it easier to hide the occasional poor hire, but the smaller organization just can not afford to make that kind of mistake. The repercussions are too costly. And you know that as soon as you compromise on selecting a person who isn't quite what you are looking for that you will receive a call from a top flight candidate the next day, so hang in there, don't rush, take your time.

Machiavelli tells us that "The first method for estimating the intelligence of a ruler is to look at the men he has around him." Although I am hesitant to draw any comparisons between rulers and Leaders there is no doubt in my mind that Leaders can be judged by the people they chose to surround themselves with. The truly effective Leaders of our time are quick to realize that surrounding themselves with the right people can significantly help them to do a far superior job than they could ever dream of doing themselves. Effective Leaders surround themselves with good people for there is no greater potential for growing an organization than to invite the right players to join the team and then to help them develop to their full potential.

Shared Expectations

From time to time I have been asked to "open up" communications between executives from the same Management Team that have drifted apart. I expect that this situation is somewhat similar to a ruptured marital relationship. Often I am faced with managers who find it increasingly difficult to really communicate any more.

As you can imagine each situation is unique, but the one consistent factor I see among these ruptured relationships is a lack of understanding of what each person expects of the other. I call this “shared expectations.”

When I refer to “shared expectations” I am really talking about a multi-step process:

1. Face-to-face discussions of what you expect of your colleague.
2. Clarification of what the expectations really mean.
3. A confirmation and commitment to the expectations.

Of course, this is a two way street. Unlike the traditional quasi-militaristic approach to Leadership in business of, “I’m the Boss, so here is what I want, now get out of here,” it is crucial that both people share and commit to the agreed expectations of the other party. Be clear on this. I am not talking about E-Mail or memos, I am talking about good old fashioned, face-to-face dialogue.

One of the challenges that people in management positions encounter is the tendency to want to manage their most valuable resource, their people, the same way that they manage things such as inventory and receivables. In an effort to achieve this, many organizations have implemented a formalized performance review process. Unfortunately, even the experts in the field of performance review are questioning their effectiveness.

By formalizing this process on an annual or semi-annual basis, many organizations are sending the message that this is the only time that a discussion of this nature can take place. The reality is that the most effective Leaders incorporate an informal performance evaluations as part of their ongoing process. Shared expectations!

Another concern that I have heard from managers, is the time that is required of a more regimented, cover your butt, dot every i kind of performance review. Some would argue “what does it really achieve?” other than distracting the organizational focus from an external focus to an internal focus. Rather than focusing on customers and opportunities, the efforts of the people are distracted to an internal, critique style perspective rather than an external perspective, focused on opportunities. One deals with the past, the other with the future.

Action Plan ... Converting Ideas Into Actions

1. What do you think the person that you report to expects of you?

2. What do you expect of the person you report to?

3. What do you expect of each of your people?

4. What do you think your people think you expect of them?

Recommendation: Get face-to-face with your associates to compare and clarify "shared expectations." As an example, what you think your manager expects of you really doesn't matter. What is critical is the reality of what your manager expects of you.

The Generation Gap

Often as I examine Leadership conflicts, what I find myself looking at is really the proverbial Generation Gap. When 40-something managers attempt to lead 20-something employees, it can pose some special challenges. The more mature managers often think that their people are looking for the same things that they wanted 20 years ago. Wrong!

So what are younger employees really looking for today? Well, to begin with, it is almost impossible to offer too much recognition, appreciation and celebration. Another primary want of young people today is to be included by spending time with their managers. And unlike the environment that many of us were conditioned in, young employees today are looking for fun. Two other key items that are on the wish list of most young people are an opportunity to learn new skills and the possibility for advancement.

On the other hand, some of the critical turnoffs that young people tell me they are looking to avoid include; workaholism, rigidity, lack of inclusion, being taken for granted, and a police state mentality style of management.

Remembering that each person is unique and doubting our efforts at mental telepathy, there is only one way to determine what is really important to anyone. Ask them and then listen. You will be amazed at what you will learn.

From *"Me"* to *"We"*

With all of the changes in the business arena over the last few years, there is no doubt that one of the most significant is the emerging role of a Manager as a "Coach." Is it any wonder? When you think of the exciting results that can be achieved through the fulfillment of what I believe a Leader's prime responsibility to be, it really shouldn't surprise us. If you are serious about "helping your people become the best that they can possibly be" then your efforts to enhance your coaching skills will pay big dividends.

Dr. Jack Weber tells us, "The bottom line is that Leadership shows up in the inspired actions of others. We traditionally have assessed Leaders themselves. Maybe we should assess Leadership by the degree to which the people around Leaders are inspired." I would take it one step further. Not only to the degree that others are inspired, but to the degree that others succeed. Successful Leaders are successful People Developers and successful People Developers are successful Coaches.

The successful Leaders of today are those who have recognized that their Number One priority, as a Leader within the organization, is to provide the coaching that their people require to become the best that they can be.

As a Leader, the more people you develop the greater the extent of your success. In order to adapt to this new reality, one that will help you produce exciting results, it is necessary to move from an Independent mindset to an Interdependent mindset. The language of "me" to the language of "we." It is only once you develop the Interdependent Leadership Skills you require, that you will be able to excel as a Coach and as a Leader. The high degree of self-sufficiency and independence that allowed you to succeed, can in fact become your own worst enemy in your efforts to move to the ultimate level of personal and professional development … Leadership.

Our experience has been that many managers who are placed in Leadership positions attempt to do it all alone. They do not focus on their responsibility to coach their people. Someday they will come to the same conclusion as the brick layer who tried to move five hundred pounds of bricks from the top of a four story building to the sidewalk below.

His problem was his inability to move from an independent mindset to an interdependent mindset. He tried to do it alone. On the insurance claim he explained exactly what happened.

> *"It would have taken too long to carry the bricks down by hand, so I decided to put them in a barrel and lower them by a pulley which I had fastened to the top of the building. After tying the rope securely at the ground level, I then went up to the top of the building. I fastened the rope around the barrel, loaded it with the bricks, and swung it out over the sidewalk for the descent. Then I went down to the sidewalk and untied the rope, holding it securely to guide the barrel down slowly. But since I weigh only one hundred and forty pounds, the five hundred pound load jerked me from the ground so fast that I didn't have time to think of letting go of the rope. And as I passed between the second and third floors, I met the barrel coming down. This accounts for the bruises and lacerations on my upper body."*
>
> *"I held on tightly to the rope until I reached the top, where my hand became jammed in the pulley. This accounts for my broken thumb. At the same time, the barrel hit the sidewalk with a bang and the bottom fell out. With the weight of the bricks gone, the barrel weighed only about forty pounds. Thus my one hundred and forty pound body began a swift descent and I met the empty barrel coming up. This accounts for my broken ankle."*
>
> *"Slowed only slightly, I continued the descent and landed on the pile of bricks. This accounts for my sprained back and broken collar bone."*
>
> *"At this point, I completely lost it and let go of the rope. The empty barrel came crashing down on me.*

This accounts for my head injuries."

"As for the last question on the form, "What would you do if the same situation arose again? Please be advised that I am finished trying to do the job alone."

I encourage you to stop trying to do it alone. Your organization is populated by a wealth of excellent people. What can you do to coach your people to greater success?

As I work with clients, one of the factors that I have been able to identify that sets the most successful firms apart from those that achieve only average or struggling results, is the ability of the members of the management team to successfully coach their people. It is the coaching that the Leaders provide that will enable their people to bloom and blossom to their full maximum potential, to become the best that they can possibly be.

While coaching is only one of many critical factors that build the Leadership puzzle, I am convinced it is a piece of the puzzle that holds great opportunity for future success.

There will be more about the exciting topic of coaching later on in this book.

Set Them Free

The Webster Dictionary describes Leadership as "showing the way by going first." Why is it that something that can be described so simply, is so difficult to achieve?

As I work with organizations across North America, there is no doubt in my mind of the magnitude of the potential for improved results that effective Leadership can produce. In fact, I doubt that any single talent is in more demand in business today, than Leadership. When you think about it, absolutely everything in your organization rises and falls on the Leadership talents of your key people.

I believe that much of the difficulty of addressing "the Leadership Famine" of today lies with the fact that the great majority of managers are modeling themselves after an inappropriate model. The model of yesterday. Now, with the world changing at breakneck speed, only a unique model of Leadership for our times will have any chance of success. The problem is this. Managers who have been conditioned by those before them are quick to adopt an independent style. This style relies heavily on control — the control of people.

A major limitation of an independent management style is that you may be able to control, to some degree, the feet and the hands of people, but you cannot have any influence over their minds and their hearts. It is in their minds and hearts that a vast wealth of untapped, discretionary power resides.

In addition, the "control thing" severely limits a manager's ability to delegate and produces barriers between people and departments. Neither does it encourage others in the organization to graduate from a dependent mindset to independence. Trapped in dependency, employees start to rot in an environment that severely limits their performance, growth, and satisfaction. Their choices are to sadly submit to a wasted life or to escape. This misplaced, burning desire for control breeds dependent employees who are focused inwardly on "the boss." What is needed today is an outward focus on solutions and the future rather than the traditional manager's mindset of problems and the past.

My experience is that independent management is not suited for the interdependent reality of business today. Independent managers who do not possess the maturity to conduct themselves interdependently may be excellent individual producers, but that is the best they will ever be.

There is no doubt that independent managers achieve

results through their own efforts. Their efforts, however, are over-shadowed by the exciting results orchestrated by interdependent Leaders. Leaders produce exciting results through the creative co-operation of all concerned. Independent people will not be able to develop their full Leadership potential until they adopt an interdependent mindset. In the interdependent business world of today, only those who adjust to the new reality will succeed as Leaders.

This revolutionary change from a quasi-militaristic management style, to a more enlightened, more effective Leadership style, can only be achieved by those who develop an interdependent mindset. The language of "we" rather than the language of "me."

By moving away from "demanding and distracting" their people, the truly effective Leaders of today succeed at "setting their people free!" Let us not underestimate the capabilities of our people. These are the same people who race home at the end of a hard work week, organize twenty, 12-year-old children on a bus, travel across an international border to a foreign city, coach six games in two days, and return home by bedtime on Sunday night with all of the original twenty children and the trophy. Yet back on the job Monday morning, the same person isn't allowed to purchase $5 worth of pencils without reams of forms and multiple signatures. Do you think that we might be short-changing ourselves about what our people are truly capable of? Just think of what your people might be able to achieve if you choose to "set them free!" Together, what could you accomplish? How far could you reach?

Action Plan ... Converting Ideas Into Actions

1. What can I do to create an environment that will enable my people to be the best they can?

2. What could I be doing to help my people to work together to discover their own solutions?

3. How could I do a better job of supporting the empowerment of my people?

4. If I was able to help my people become more empowered, what kind of impact could it have on our organization?

The Ultimate Leadership Mindset

As I work with Leaders in all kinds of organizations, a common theme echoed by the management is, "Ross, why won't our people be more responsible?" Unfortunately, the answer to this question often lies with the managers themselves. My experience has been that your people will not make this empowering shift until they feel it is safe to do so. In order for your people to develop the trust that they need to assume that more responsible role that you are hoping for them to step into, they need to be encouraged, appreciated and included. It is these positive feelings, these "good vibes," that will help you to build the trust with your people that is the basis of a more powerful organization. But before we ask our people to shift their mindset, it is important that we participate in some mental adjustments of our own.

As a business person and entrepreneur, I have recognized that much of my personal success is as a result of the independent mindset that I have developed. This independent mindset is characterized by a high sense of personal responsibility. Not wanting to rely on others, my independent mindset would tell me that "if it is to be, it is up to me."

This independent mindset that I refer to is what got most of us to the Leadership positions that we are in today. As our results improved and as our confidence built, we climbed the corporate ladder. Now that I have had an opportunity to study effective Leaders the way that I have, I realize that the Independent mindset that got me here isn't good enough if I am to graduate to the next level of personal and professional growth. In fact, the characteristics and attributes that are driven by my independent mindset could very well become my enemies. It is easy to stop growing and park ourselves in the independent mode with all of its comfort and security. But if you are to succeed as a Leader it is critical that you develop a mindset that is in alignment with the new reality of today. An interdependent reality.

Think of it? Here we are with thousands of organizations that are populated by independently minded managers attempting to fulfill their Leadership role in an interdependent business reality. Is it any wonder that North American businesses experience the lack of achievement that they do in contrast to the magnitude of the incredible potential? Managers trapped in an independent mindset. And what do we hear from their people; "My manager just won't delegate." "My manager doesn't care what we have to say." "My manager won't listen." "My manager keeps us in the dark." All of these comments are typical of descriptions of an independently oriented manager. An independent manager who is out of alignment with the reality of today. An interdependent reality.

Without a doubt, what is needed to achieve as an effective Leader today, is to shift from the traditional independent mindset to interdependence. Interdependence - the ability to work together co-operatively to help those around you to achieve everything that they are truly capable of.

By now, as an independent manager, you are probably already starting to notice the limitations and the frustrations that independence can produce. You know that there has to be a better way. You just don't know what it is. While the characteristics and attributes of independence served you well in that they got you where you are, I can guarantee you that if you now find yourself in a Leadership role, these same qualities are not good enough to keep you where you are, let alone allow you to continue to experience new successes.

The independent mindset is about control. You may be

able to control things but you won't be able to control people. There is an important point of differentiation here. The quote that I use to best describe this critical point is, "Manage things, Lead people." You may be able to control to some minor degree the hands and backs of people but is that what we are really looking for today? Of course not. As Leaders your success or failure lies in your ability to access the wealth of untapped human potential that resides in the hearts and minds of your people.

I believe that the independent mindset of a manager can be doubly dangerous. Not only does it hinder the Leader's ability to help his or her people achieve all that they are capable of through the release of all of that untapped human potential but at the same time it traps others in the dependency mode. Often what I see is a strong willed, independent manager who surrounds himself with dependent people. In fact, if the people don't start out dependent in this kind of environment they are often conditioned to adapt to the dependency mode. This dependency on the manager negatively impacts performance, growth, satisfaction and quickly brings the pace of the organization to a standstill.

Is it any wonder that organizations, managed by independently minded people, struggle the way that they do? Their tendency to always want to have the answer, their aversion to listening, their need to be personally involved in even the most minor decisions, and their compelling desire to "control" people the same way that they control things is not a recipe for success.

You can imagine what can happen when you have an organization where the predominant style of the department managers is independence. What do you think the relationships between the departments might look like? Yet think about how interdependent departments really are. If you were able to convert your organization from the independent, competitive model that independent management breeds, to the interdependent corporation that interdependent Leadership creates, what kind of impact would it have on your people, and your success? What kind of inter-department barriers would be destroyed? How would the destruction of these barriers to success impact the profitability of your operations? Imagine your entire organization functioning in an environment of creative co-operation across the entire span of your operations. Together, what could you accomplish?

In order to achieve the kinds of shifts that many of us are asking our people to make, it is absolutely mandatory that you set the pace and clear the way by graduating from an independent mindset to a mindset based on interdependence.

How does one initiate this shift from independence to interdependence? My experience has been that just recognizing the need to change is a big part of the solution. However, good intentions are not enough to achieve the kind of quantum leaps forward that we are proposing here.

Personally, I would recommend Stephen Covey's book, "The Seven Habits of Highly Effective People" as an excellent start. Covey does the best job that I have seen in dealing with the shift from independence to interdependence.

In order to be an effective Leader, I have identified the areas that I need to make adjustments in. I share these with you, not so you duplicate what I have done, but rather for you to consider how you may develop your own affirmations.

"As an interdependent Leader functioning in an interdependent reality I will only be able to enjoy all the benefits of success when I:

1. open up to people and show them the real me rather than playing the corporate role that I think is expected of me.

2. trust my associates enough to stop trying to control them.

3. realize that I don't need to be right all of the time.

4. recognize that I don't need to have all the answers all of the time."

Again, this is my own personal affirmation that is designed to help me develop as a Leader. Only you know what is going to work best for you. I encourage you to invest the time to script an affirmation along these lines. Personally, I can tell you that my affirmation has a very positive impact on my ability to Lead. Without it, I doubt that I could be as focused as I am, and at the same time it does an excellent job of reminding me of my weaknesses which in itself is a very humbling experience. Isn't that a big part of what we are talking about? To shift from the traditional ego-driven, task oriented manager to a more humble, people oriented approach to Leadership–Macho to Maestro!

Action Plan ... Converting Ideas Into Action

1. How would your people see you? Dependent? Independent? or Interdependent?

2. What are some of the things you could do to better establish yourself as a Leader in the Interdependent Style?

3. If you were able to achieve this, what might some of the results be?

Wandering Around

Some of the most successful Leaders I have had the pleasure to work with, are absolutely ruthless about making themselves available and "wandering around." This is the alternative to a formal, more traditional, structured approach to meetings.

I just love it when I call a client and I am told that they are not available, that they are "wandering around." This kind of, what appears to be, aimless wandering around can be powerful. As opposed to isolating yourself in one corner of a building, "wandering around" sends a real message to all concerned that you are there to help them. It is the Supportive Style rather than the Superiority Style of Leadership. Supportive Leadership is characterized by what I call the "Helping Habit," wanting to help your people achieve all that they are truly capable of. My experience has been that the most successful organizations I have had an opportunity to work with are populated by Leaders who practice the Art and Science of "Wandering Around."

Meeting Madness

It has been my fortune to observe Leaders at work and play for over twenty years now. In this time, my inspiration has come from the examples I have gathered as I have worked with and observed Leaders in action. Some are good examples. Some are not so good, but one thing that is for certain is that I have learned a lot of interesting things from observing others.

I have never been a big fan of needless, excessive meetings, so my opinions in this area are drawn from watching others and seeing what works best for them. There is no doubt about the valid purposes that meetings can play in any organization. Nothing can replace good old-fashioned, face to face dialogue and the understanding and synergy that it is capable of producing.

Unfortunately far too many organizations have taken meetings to an extreme. It seems that in some organizations everyone is constantly in meetings–Meeting Madness! Internal meetings isolate people from the reality of the business world that they function in. Unfortunately these companies that are "meetingized to death" are suffering from a severe lack of Leadership. Excessive meetings lead to the fatal disease of management by committee.

I know that participatory management is a popular buzz word these days, but be careful. What does participatory management mean to you? If your brand of participatory management includes countless meetings and committees that paralyze your operations, my recommendation would be that you find a better way. Would you want a participatory style of management if you were a passenger in an out-of-control 747 crashing to the ground? Have you heard the joke about the definition of a camel? A horse designed by a committee. The words committee and compromise are just too close to each other in the dictionary. In today's world we need to seek out the best solutions and strategies, not weak compromises based on appeasing all of the participants.

So here is one symptom of poor or ineffective Leadership. Does it seem as if all of the key people in your organization are constantly in a never ending loop of meetings? Once you reach a certain level in terms of frequency of meetings and time spent in meetings, the diminishing law of marginal returns kicks in. In fact, how appropriate do you think the Pareto Principle (the 80/20 rule) is to the meetings in your organization? Does 20% of the time you invest in meetings produce 80% of the results?

I encourage Leaders that I have worked with to abide by six rules when it comes to meetings:

1. If you are in a meeting for more than 10 minutes without anyone mentioning customers, be quick to point this out to the group.

2. If after an additional 5 minutes, you still are not talking about customers get up and walk out.

3. If one of your people requests to meet with you, arrange to do so in their office. Do not let anybody drag their problems down the hall to your office.

4. Let your colleagues know that you will not take responsibility for any of their problems. They can not abandon their problems with you. Of course, you will be interested and available to discuss any issues and potential solutions with them.

5. When you are in a meeting don't be afraid to quantify the value of the talent you have gathered in the room and compare it to the magnitude of the issues being discussed. As an example, 10 members of a management team with an overhead rate of $200 per hour, per person, better be certain that the issues they are discussing have significant payback opportunities compared to the $2000. per hour cost of the meeting.

6. Listen, listen, listen. For a Leader, meetings can be a great opportunity to tune into what is really happening in your organization.

Playing To Win

In today's competitive markets, it is critical that as a Leader you strive to develop a "Playing to Win" mindset within yourself and among all of your associates. This mindset is diametrically opposed to the model that I believe a high percentage of managers and organizations practice which is "Playing not to Lose."

Playing not to lose is about safety and comfort. In society today there exists two major motivators. Pain and pleasure. Of these two, pain is the more powerful. People will do just about anything to avoid pain. People who play not to lose are driven by the desire to avoid the pain of emotional discomfort, the pain of rejection, the pain of failure, and the pain of making a mistake. If you or your organization is trapped in the playing not to lose model, you could be missing out on incredible opportunities. It may be very safe to park on the sidelines but let me assure you that the new reality will pass you by very quickly.

On the other hand, by utilizing the courage and the creativity of your people to support an organization based on a playing to win model, you will start to see exciting things happen immediately. It is about taking risks, facing new challenges, and discovering new opportunities. It is about experiencing life to the fullest by breaking out of our comfort zones. Remember, "One hundred percent of the shots that you do not take, will never score!"

Let me ask you this. Mentally, where do you reside? Do you live in the past, the present or the future? My own estimate is that a very small percentage, maybe 10% of us live in the present. Is it really possible to live in the past or the future? Of course not, but think of all the brain cells that are drained worrying about past or future issues.

One of the keys to helping your organization adopt a "Play to Win" culture is to move away from the traditional critique mode of management. You know what I mean because I bet you have heard it hundreds of times. Rather than celebrate the $100,000. order, we are quick to critique why we were not able to capture all of the business when the customer selected the competition to supply them with one or two of the smaller items. Critique, critique, critique. What I often see is "No celebration, No appreciation, No recognition, and then critique, critique, critique."

A manager who is often in the critique mode is desperately trapped in the past. In fact, if a Leader's responsibility is to guide his or her people into the future, the critique mode is doubly dangerous. Not only does it create a culture based on what is wrong but it also ensures that nobody is performing the critical function of looking into the future. If you sense that you occasionally have been trapped in a critique mindset, I encourage you to act immediately to escape.

If your people are not taking risks, that is scary enough. But what is even scarier is if your competition is taking risks that are accelerating them into the future. I often see organizations parked in neutral, relishing their past glories, while the new players in their markets are creating the future. By the time the established, more dominant player realizes that reality has raced past them, the competition has such a lead that it is difficult to even play catch-up. In business, we really do it to ourselves don't we?

Teams

We all are familiar with traditional organizations build on the pyramid model. This model may have worked well in a different time, but the new reality of today just doesn't allow for the kinds of inefficiencies that come with this traditional model. Layers and layers of managers and supervisors serve as barriers to the free flow of communications and kill both energy and creativity in any organization. Look at the firms you know that are built on this model and you will start to wonder how they have been able to survive this long, even if they are just limping along.

With the dismantling of these traditional bureaucracies comes a move to teamwork. In the interdependent world that we function in, it is critical that we build an interdependence in our own organizations. There just isn't room for Lone Ranger managers or departments anymore. We are all dependent on each other and one of the best ways of building a high level of interdependence is to adopt a team culture.

One of the challenges of discussing teams is that there are so many different models and each of us could have a different definition of what a team really is. My paradigm for a team is a pride of lions. The pride succeeds because it is led by a strong Leader and at the same time it is composed of motivated, contributing individuals who work together to achieve common goals. Unlike a more socialistic definition of teams that I often hear about, in the lion pride weakness is simply not tolerated. In business, if all of the players are not contributing, the entire team could be in jeopardy. How long would a baseball team tolerate a short stop who routinely misses balls hit in his direction?

Just as a lion pride needs a Leader and a professional sports team needs a Leader, so do the successful teams of business. An effective Leader who can balance the need for decisive decisions with the need to empower the members of the team to create innovative, new ideas.

Just as in sports, it is not easy to build a powerful, well run team in business, but the benefits of doing so make the efforts well worth while. How does one go about building a team? Some of the key coaching skills that you will want to keep in mind include the creation of a shared vision for the team and the development of specific goals that will contribute to the team's success. It is vital that these goals are team oriented rather than individual goals, otherwise you will be seen as talking out of both sides of your mouth. If you are really serious about teams you need to reinforce this commitment to the team's success through team goals that support co-operation in the workplace, not competition. In addition, each member of your team needs to know that their contribution really counts and their efforts are appreciated. Be quick to celebrate the success of the team, but make certain that when things go wrong that you don't start finger pointing in public. No longer is it good enough for team Leaders in business to isolate themselves in an Ivory Tower. Teams by their basic definition need their Leaders right there with them, down on the sidelines or in the dugout, experiencing both the agony of defeat and the joy of success.

In their book "Teamwork: What Must Go Right/What Can Go Wrong" the authors, Larson and LaFasto tell us that "Effective Leaders give team members the self-confidence to act, to take charge of their responsibilities, and make changes occur rather than merely perform assigned tasks. In short, Leaders create Leaders!" In business, as in sports, successful teams create dynasties. When all is said and done, each organization is a team with all of the employees, including the executive, the managers, and the workers being judged by one criteria, the success of the organization. As obvious as the need for enhanced teamwork in organizations today may be, one of my greatest disappointments is the lack of teamwork I see. Success in organizations, just like success in sports, is all about teamwork and the sooner more people start realizing it and start doing something about it, the better off we will all be. Good teams are capable of achieving good things. Good teams with effective Leadership are capable of achieving great things!

Successors

In my mind, there may be no greater indication of the failure of a Leader, than the lack of a successor. Yet how often do you see an individual leave a position of Leadership and the organization has to go outside of their own firm to replace the person. How sad! What does this really tell us about that person's Leadership talent?

Organizations succeed or fail on their ability to develop their own wealth of Leadership talent. As a Leader, one of your primary priorities should be the development of your emerging Leaders. If you do not have any emerging Leaders, you would want to start asking some questions about your hiring policies. Within your organization, who are the people that you are targeting and mentoring for future Leadership roles. Far too often people in positions of Leadership abandon their responsibilities to develop a pool of emerging Leaders. In doing so these people are really jeopardizing the future of their organization.

Within your organization who do you trust to replace you? If you have to think for more than a few nanoseconds to respond to this question, then let me suggest that you may be dropping the ball on one of your primary priorities as a Leader. The development of the emerging Leaders within your organization.

Action Plan ... Converting Ideas Into Action

1. Who are the people in your organization who could be considered as possible successors to your job?

2. For each of these people, what kind of help can you offer to better qualify them as an excellent candidate for your position.

Shared Vision ... Converting Vision Into Reality

Isn't it amazing how quickly tomorrow arrives? The future is rapidly rushing straight at us at breakneck speed, and it is in this chaotic environment that the successful Leaders of today must maintain their focus on the future. Peter Drucker tells us that "The best way to predict the future is to create it." With so many possibilities facing any organization and the future arriving on our doorsteps so quickly, it is vital that the Leaders remain focused on the future.

One of my personal tests of Leadership effectiveness that I apply when visiting a new prospective client is to ask the members of the management team about the future. Often what I hear is a disjointed conversation with some of the managers stumbling this way and others wandering another direction in their thoughts. What I often sense is that this is the first time that they have ever endeavored to collectively develop a vision of their future. As managers, they are either desperately trying to re-create the past or to solve the urgent issues of the present rather than focusing on the exciting opportunities of the future. If the Leaders are not focused on the future, I have to wonder what the future holds for their organization. One thing is for certain, their future will be whatever and wherever events take them rather than a specific chosen destination.

The role of the Leader is all about the future. Leroy Eims, the author of "Be The Leader You Were Meant To Be" describes it this way; "A Leader is one who sees more than others see, who sees farther than others see, and who sees before others do." More, farther, and before. Similarly Kouzes and Posner in their book "The Leadership Challenge" point out the "Leaders are pioneers. They are people who venture into unexplored territory. They guide us to new and often unfamiliar destinations. People who take the lead are the foot soldiers in the campaigns for change ... the unique reason for having Leaders—their differentiating function—is to move forward. Leaders get us going someplace." If we do not know where we are going we will probably not like where we arrive. Let's make certain that we enjoy not only the destination but also the entire journey.

Time and time again, as I meet with successful Leaders, they consistently identify that one of the major factors that has contributed to the success of their organizations is the fact that they have worked with their colleagues to develop a vision of the future. The results of establishing visions and goals are incredible. I am constantly amazed by the magnitude of the success stories. I know that in my own life, my experience has been that whenever I have set goals, not only do I achieve them, but often the goals are reached in a much faster time frame than expected. Is there any reason that the same should not hold true for organizational goals?

In establishing goals that will contribute to the success of achieving your vision, it is important that your goals are meaningful. They should be both achievable and exciting. If possible, you will find it helpful to affix a time frame to your organizational goals. This will help you avoid allowing your goals to drift off into dreams. A goal without a deadline is nothing but a dream.

Once you and your associates have worked together to establish your vision of the future for your organization, you will start to notice a big difference. Your people will know where you are leading them. There will be no suspicions that you are wandering aimlessly, lost in the desert of destiny. With that vision clearly understood, your people will develop a burning desire to excel. After all, it just does not make sense to be running on full throttle if you aren't certain of your destination.

By planting the seeds of a new vision, you will be ensuring a bountiful harvest for all of your people. As a Leader, just the simple act of showing willingness to create a new vision communicates a strong message about your belief in the ability of your people and their potential. By creating a new vision, you, as a Leader, will look into the future with positive anticipation of good things to come rather than nervous apprehension–possibilities not problems. If you feel that way you can bet that your people have similar feelings.

Another advantage that successful Leaders point out to me is that a new vision of the future serves to help you escape from the limitations of the past and opens you up to exciting possibilities in the future. Many Leaders tell me that they and their people would be lost if they did not have a clearly stated, well understood vision to focus on. There is a key word ... focus. With so many opportunities available to each person, and to every organization, it is critical that we focus our efforts.

Louis Lundborg, the former Chairman of the Bank of America put it this way. "Success ... my nomination for the single most important ingredient is energy well directed."

In other words "focus!" Just think about this for a moment. If you and your people are not focused, where are you? If you are not on target, you are off target and how long can you survive without hitting the bull's eye?

The new reality is one of lean and mean resources. I don't know about you, but none of my clients have people sitting around waiting for something to do. We just can't afford to waste our resources if we are to survive, let alone thrive. A shared vision of the future provides everyone concerned with a common target, something to shoot for. If your people are not focusing on your bull's eye, if they are distracted from the target, their contributions to your success will be diluted. It just isn't enough to be busy anymore. The real questions is what are we busy doing? Are we focused on the bull's eye? Are our efforts hitting the target?

You may have heard the story about the three bricklayers working together on the same project. Despite the fact that all three bricklayers worked with the same tools, mortar and bricks, a passer-by sensed that there was something different. Curious to discover more, the passer-by inquired of the first worker, "What are you doing?"

"Laying bricks," came the answer. "It's a hard job but somebody has to do it."

"What is it that you are doing?" the passer-by asked the second worker.

"I am part of this construction crew and we are working on the west wall of this structure."

"And what is that you are doing ?" the passer-by asked the third bricklayer?

"I am helping to build a glorious cathedral," replied the man, "and when we are finished the alter will stand right where you are standing and people from all over will come to meet and worship."

What are the differences that you observed between the bricklayers? What usually jumps out at people are the differences between the attitudes of the bricklayers. The first worker had a job. The second worker was involved in a common goal. The third worker had developed a clear vision of the future. And just think of the kind of impact that shared vision of the future can have on your people? There really is a world of difference between laying bricks and building a cathedral. As a Leader, which do you choose for your people and your organization?

Some people are quick to challenge me on the importance that I place on the creation of a shared vision of the future. They ask me why is it that I am so interested in the future. I borrow my response from the words of Charles Kettering who said, "My interest is in the future because I am going to spend the rest of my life there." How about you?

Action Plan ... Converting Ideas Into Action

1. When you look at your organization, what is your vision of the future?

2. Is your vision shared with your associates?

3. How focused are your people on the vision of the future for your business.

4. What are some of the advantages that you might enjoy if all of your people focused on a shared vision of the future?

Advanced Communication Skills For Leadership

"Better communications!" I know they are buzz words, but at the same time we all realize the incredible potential that better communications hold for those of us in Leadership roles. But just realizing it isn't enough! Certainly awareness is part of the answer to the communication famine that we experience in our organizations today, but the big rewards come from the application and utilization of specific communication skills. This chapter is designed to introduce you to advanced communication skills in two critical areas. The first area of communications that I address are specific listening skills, and the second area deals with the development of an effective questioning strategy. Together this arsenal of communications skills will enhance your effectiveness as a Leader.

Ben Franklin, the great American statesman tells us that "people are best convinced by reasons that they themselves discover." How do you feel when somebody tells you what to do? When we tell people what to do there is often a strong tendency to resist. This is true no matter how wonderful your ideas are. Most people just don't want to be told what to do and how to do it. Yet how does the traditional manager spend most of his or her time? Telling people what to do and how to do it. Is it any wonder that our efforts to communicate often fail the way that they do? One of the most closely held human emotions is the need to be heard and understood. And the three things that people want to talk about the most? Themselves, themselves and themselves. Yet, seldom do we give people the opportunity to tell us what they are thinking or how they are feeling.

The ideas that people will throw themselves behind are the ones that they develop themselves. The key here is inclusion and commitment. Together these two forces will combine to produce some exciting results from the experts on the challenges facing your organization—your very own people. An ancient Chinese proverb says "Tell me and I'll forget; show me and I may remember; involve me and I'll understand." Not only will I understand, but I will be totally committed. Never underestimate the awesome force of inclusion.

As you know, people don't resist change as much as they resist being made to change. When we are in our telling mode we are really trying to force change on others. Telling will guarantee you two reactions. Defensiveness and resistance. Now how successful can you be as a Leader when you are functioning in a mode that is creating defensiveness and resistance?

In addition to a high degree of commitment, a second benefit of inclusion is that others often come up with some wonderfully creative ideas. Ideas that you alone wouldn't even start to think of. It is in a synergistic environment of creative co-operativeness that alternatives are often discovered.

In order to become a successful Leader you need to become passionately obsessed with the need to communicate as effectively as possible. Here then are some communications skills that have helped others enhance their Leadership effectiveness. Perhaps they can do the same for you.

Versatility

If you are Leading people in a style that is natural to yourself, you may be wasting as much as half of your time and half of your efforts. This is a frightening thought for anyone in a Leadership role. Developing a knowledge of Behavioral Styles will help you make the most of your time and effort when communicating.

In this section I will accomplish three things. First, I will help you understand your own style and allow you to see yourself as your people see you. Secondly, I will help you learn to quickly and accurately pinpoint the styles of others. Thirdly, I will show you how you can utilize your knowledge of Behavioral Styles to communicate with others as effectively as possible. Your ability to properly manage your personal style may very well have a more positive impact on your Leadership ability than any other single communications skill. You will see that the results will be both immediate and powerful. Skill with Behavioral Styles will dramatically assist you in your professional Leadership role. It will also help you build positive relations outside of work.

Your success as a Leader is not determined by your style, and certainly there is much more to Leadership than this one communication skill. In fact there is no right or wrong style, no best style for Leadership. The key to utilizing styles to enhance your Leadership effectiveness is versatility. By this I mean the versatility that you demonstrate in order to allow others to remain in their own "comfort zones." It is only when people are in their own "comfort zone" that they will be receptive and open-minded to new ideas–your ideas. Your ability to maintain a high level of trust and comfort between yourself and others will have a very positive impact on your success as a Leader.

There are two key factors that will reveal a person's style to you. The first is Responsiveness. Responsiveness is the person's desire to show emotions. The second key factor is Assertiveness. Assertiveness is a persons' desire to control others. Of course we all have degrees of both responsiveness and assertiveness.

It is possible for us to observe the traits of others and, based on what we see, estimate the degree of responsiveness and assertiveness. This mixture results in four distinct styles. Expressives, Drivers, Analyticals and Amiables. Because we all vary in degree it is possible for a person to be a blend of each. Responsive people are people oriented, while an assertive person is task oriented.

This section is not intended to serve as an in-depth discussion of styles but rather to be an introduction to what I believe is a critical communication skill. Styles are really about versatility and we all show varying degrees of versatility when dealing with others. If you are already very sensitive to the topic of styles then this brief description serves as an excellent reminder of a skill that is already working for you. If on the other hand styles are a concept that is new to you then perhaps we will capture your curiosity. If styles are of interest to you, I would recommend that you read more on this subject or that you participate in a styles workshop.

Some of the major identifiable traits of each characteristic are:

RESPONSIVENESS

HIGH	**LOW**
Relaxed	Formal
Warm	Proper
Informal	Guarded

ASSERTIVENESS

HIGH	**LOW**
No time	Excess of time
Uses people	Serves others
Works for goals	Hides behind work

On the chart below identify the style that you think does the best job of describing yourself. Once you have identified your own style familiarize yourself with the other styles so that you can see how other people prefer to be treated.

Of special importance is the style that is diagonal to your own. These people prefer things that are very different from you so there is a strong likelihood of tension in your relationship with them. Again, versatility can be the solution.

AMIABLES	**EXPRESSIVES**
are less time disciplined	have big dreams
like to work carefully	use hunches to decide
like to build relationships	like to be with people
like to minimize risks	often make quick decisions
enjoy the traditional	like to plan for the future
like to be appreciated	are less time disciplined
are supportive	take risks
enjoy working in groups	need to receive approval and recognition

ANALYTICALS	**DRIVERS**
work carefully	like to be on time
use facts and data	work very quickly
work independently	take risks
are organized	like to be given choices
like to be on time	use power
focus on detail	would rather work independently
need to be right	focus on results now
want to minimize risks	

If you are uncertain about a person's style think about how they reacted the last time you observed them under stress. Based on my experience I would expect to see expressives attack, amiables go along, analyticals avoid and drivers to become autocratic.

I guarantee people will find something wrong with your message if they find something wrong with you. In order to ensure that you are communicating with open and receptive minds, it is important to show versatility in your actions. As simple as these versatile actions can be, they go a long way towards ensuring that you are working "in alignment" with others rather than "out of alignment."

So what are some of the versatile actions that we can take to help others feel comfortable with us and in turn to ensure a receptive mind?

When communicating with **Analyticals**, it is important to slow your speech pace and moderate your vocal inflections. You would want to be focused on the details and offer whatever assurance you can to ensure that the Analytical person is not exposed to risk. In addition, you would want to conduct yourself in a very businesslike manner.

With **Drivers** you need to remember that they are looking for results and they usually want those results yesterday. Your pace should be quick and you should control your emotions. Don't waste time, stay on target and be efficient. A businesslike approach is appreciated here.

When communicating with people of the **Amiable** style you would want to show a high degree of personal interest in order to support the relationship. You should take whatever time is required. It is important to be casual and informal and to work at a slower more relaxed pace. Amiables feel uncomfortable with a high degree of risk so anything you might be able to do to provide assurances would be appreciated. If there is one thing that characterizes what the amiable is looking for, it is the personal relationship.

With the **Expressive** you would want to be more "wild and crazy" than with the other styles. Fast paced, stimulating conversation will serve you well here. Expressives feel uncomfortable with the details so stay focused on the "big picture" and be certain to provide liberal doses of recognition and approval which means constant stroking of their ego.

One final point on versatility. Your increased sensitivity to styles will help you to see others in a very different light. Styles are not about "why isn't that person like me?" but rather are about appreciating and admiring the differences in others. It is the combined perspectives of the different styles that will often allow us to find the best solution.

Listening To Lead

When it comes to listening, just an awareness of the importance of listening is a big part of the solution. My experience of working with Leaders has been that the most significant results come from the application of specific listening skills. Lets' take a look at some of the listening skills that have been able to help others.

If there is one quote that relates more to the importance of listening in a Leadership role than any other, it would have to be the one that my wife Charleen often reminds me of. "If you are talking, all that you are doing is repeating something that you already know. If you are listening, you may learn something new." As Leaders, it is critical that we are constantly gathering and evaluating new information about topics such as our people, our organization, our markets. As long as our lips are moving we are not learning anything new, we are simply repeating what we already know.

I have always found it ironical that the North American education system has devoted itself to Reading and Writing. At the same time, it has totally ignored the role that listening plays in creating effective communications. Recently I asked some of my clients to monitor and report to me the amount of time that they spend reading, writing and listening. Amazingly enough, all of the Leaders reported very similar findings. These Leaders estimated that they spend less than 20% of their time either reading or writing and in excess of 80% of their time either listening or being listened to. With such a large percentage of our work being dependent on listening, I believe that it deserves more attention than the education system has given it in the past.

More and more, I realize that success comes to those firms that compete based on speed. This emphasis on speed relies heavily on a system of business communications. These communications are dependent on the spoken word more than the written word, and the effectiveness of the spoken word hinges not so much on how people talk, as how they listen. There is no doubt in my mind that the most successful Leaders are skilled listeners. How important is listening to you and your success? How well do you think others would tell us you listen?

It is not just good enough to acknowledge the importance of listening. How can you become a more effective listener? What skills will help you become a better, active listener? Active listening is the type of listening that brings success in Leadership. Take a moment and reflect on this question. As a Leader, if you were able to become a better listener, what kind of impact could it have on you personally?

The unfortunate reality is that too many organizations and individuals still believe that "glibness" is a major contributor to the success of Leaders. These organizations channel their efforts to improving the "talking" side of their managers. Based on my experience, it is my conviction that for the typical manager, the ability to talk will almost certainly take care of itself. The real opportunity for improved Leadership effectiveness lies in the area of improving specific listening skills. In the new reality of today, listening has become an essential tool for any Leader. At the same time, his or her vocal agility has become less important.

If Leadership is about influencing others then perhaps there is no greater single piece of wisdom than Stephen Covey's master communication skill of life. Covey's fifth habit of highly effective people is "Seek first to understand and then to be understood." Personally I have extended this wise advice by adding "Listen not just to respond but rather listen to truly understand." In my mind this deeply rooted commitment to "really understanding" is the essence of all professionalism.

This kind of effective listening will help you to achieve two significant results. The first is that you will be able to gather more information about what is really happening in your organization. This is the functional benefit. The second benefit of effective listening is the message that you are sending to your people. That you really do value their opinions and are keenly interested in hearing more about what they think. Your people will feel understood, included and appreciated.

One of the most beneficial listening skills you will ever encounter is to control what I call Talkitis. Talkitis is the compelling desire we all have to talk before we are ready to listen. We all suffer from this disease from one degree to another. If you can learn to recognize and control Talkitis in yourself you will be able to develop into a far more successful Leader.

It is our strong emotions that cause us to blurt out our messages, comments and complaints. The stronger the emotion, the harder it is for us to shut up or to control our compelling desire to talk. Some of the most prevalent causes of Talkitis include; defending oneself, displeasure, questions, enthusiasm and silence.

As professionals we are all proud of what we have achieved. If somebody says something that questions our competence or our decisions we quickly jump to our defense and start talking. Our Talkitis has exploded and our lips start flapping. I am sure that you have seen plenty of examples where displeasure or anger creates Talkitis. If somebody is angry at us we often respond in a like manner and start talking.

Enthusiasm, or our eagerness to get our primary message on the table, often causes us to miss hearing what the other person is trying to communicate. Enthusiasm can be doubly dangerous. You are excited about an idea and you start talking. The other person hears something that excites them and they start talking. Who is listening?

Questions pose a special problem to those of us in Leadership roles who are technically rich. We hear a question and our tendency is to answer it frankly with facts and figures. This response can be deadly as you may not have heard the real question yet. In fact, many questions are used to camouflage concerns or objections. The best strategy here is to seek to clarify the question.

We all know how silence can drive up our desire to speak. But it could be that the other person simply needs an additional second or two to formulate their thoughts and if we succumb to our Talkitis, we are interrupting their process. How do you feel when someone interrupts you?

If you sense that you are suffering from Talkitis the only logical strategy is to stop talking. Sometimes in conversations with others I find that just recognizing the need to control my Talkitis and stop talking isn't enough so I go to

Plan B. I physically grasp my tongue between my teeth. Don't laugh. It works. If I didn't take this action I would blurt out and interrupt the other person in mid-sentence and you can imagine what kind of impact that can have on effective communications.

If you see Talkitis in others it is best to let them do exactly what they are already doing–talk. It is only once their Talkitis starts to run down that their minds will be open and receptive to your ideas.

Another helpful listening skill that other Leaders tell me works well for them is a concept called Lo/Lo. The human mind can only think of one primary thought at a time. I am certain that you have been in situations where somebody has said something that has captured your attention and you have "Locked on" to it and "Locked out" the rest of what the other person is continuing to say. Lo/Lo! All that you are really doing is focusing on your own thoughts and waiting for the other person's lips to stop moving so you can jump in with your ideas.

Some of the symptoms that could indicate to you that the other person is suffering Lo/Lo, that they have stopped listening and are locked into their thoughts, include fidgeting, staring off into the distance, a shifting of their body posture or clearing their throat. When do people clear their throat? Right, just before they talk. If you see any of the symptoms of Lo/Lo, the best thing to do is to stop talking. The other person is not listening anyway. You don't even have to ask them a question since they are just waiting for your lips to stop moving so that they can jump in.

A good strategy that seems to work well to avoid Lo/Lo in yourself as you are talking with others is that if something captures your imagination, rather than falling into the Lo/Lo trap, just make a quick, simple notation of it on a pad of paper. This will help you to recall it later. This strategy ensures that as a Leader you are able to avoid Lo/Lo and focus on what people are saying.

Another listening skill that has worked well for others is called Golden Silence. A study of business conversations took a look at the average elapsed time between a person asking a question and then doing one of two things. Either asking another question or answering the question they just asked of the other person. How long do you think elapsed between the first activity and one of the other two? Would you believe something like 9/10th of a second. What kind of listening is really taking place in business? Are we listening just to respond rather than to really understand? By responding in such a quick fashion, what kind of message are we sending to the other person?

Golden Silence is the solution. It is the critical pause for a few seconds at two specific points. After you ask a question and after the other person responds. These few seconds will go a long way to creating a climate of effective communications. By introducing these two kinds of pauses into your conversations, you will dramatically improve the quality of the information that you receive from others and at the same time show, that as a Leader, you really do care about the other person's opinions.

The reasons are simple. When you practice Golden Silence by giving others a moment to think about what you have asked them, the information you receive in return will be of a higher quality.

By waiting after the other person speaks, you are giving yourself a better opportunity to understand what they have told you. The combined results of using Golden Silence, after you have asked a question and after others speak, will be a more thoughtful and more productive exchange of ideas.

A concern that some Leaders have confessed to me is

that if they are not talking, they believe that they have lost control. This condition arises from the confusion between "controlling" and "dominating" discussions. In business, it is the person who does the most talking who is dominating the discussions. But it is the person who is doing the listening who is actually in control. One of the keys to Leadership is listening. I encourage you to ruthlessly control the discussion by listening.

A fourth listening skill that compliments what we have talked about already is a concept that I call the "Three Party Conversation." Whenever you are talking with somebody else there are really three conversations taking place. There is the public conversation that we see and hear. There is a second conversation taking place in the back of the other person's mind and then there is a third conversation that you are having with yourself. Three conversations! Of the three which do you think has the most potential for you as a Leader? The conversation taking place in the other person's mind. Short of mental telepathy, my experience has been that the only way to discover what the other person is really thinking is to ask them.

A simple rule of thumb that seems to work well for other Leaders is to never talk for more than two minutes without giving others the opportunity to participate. If you don't employ this strategy you could loose your audience and your people could start to drift into Lo/Lo.

The kinds of questions I am suggesting here are the nice big, soft, fluffy ones that allow the other person enough room to tell you what is really on their mind. Examples would include "Tell me what you are thinking?" and "How does that sound to you?" These are great questions that let other people tell you what they are thinking and which are an excellent substitute for mental telepathy.

Time and time again, I hear back from Leaders who

want to tell me how well these communications skills work, not only in their professional life, but at home in their personal life. I can not tell you how many senior executives have told me the great ideas their people were able to share with them once they were given the opportunity. Not only do you benefit from new ideas, but you also communicate a very real sense of being heard, understood, included and appreciated.

With all of the good things listening has going for it, I am still amazed that it is only the wisest, most effective Leaders who choose to lead with their ears. When it comes to Leadership, and in fact, in all of life, listening really is a very big deal! Listening and Leadership go hand in hand.

Listening is really about others. At the same time, talking is often about ourselves. No other communication skill will assist you in a shift from an independent Leadership style to an interdependent Leadership style the way that listening will. The language of "me" to the language of "we." It is only once we are listening and really hearing what our people are saying that we can lay claim to having graduated to the ultimate level of Leadership.

Action Plan ... Converting Ideas Into Action

1. How important a role does communication play in your success as a Leader?

2. On a scale of 0 - 10, where do you think most of your people would score your communication skills?

3. If there was one or two areas of communication that held the most opportunity for your own personal growth, what might they be?

4. If you were able to enhance your communication skills, what kind of results might you expect?

Your Most Valuable Asset - Yourself

As a keen observer of Leadership "wellness," let me share with you some of the things that I have seen others do to bring a greater sense of balance into their lives. To a large degree, bringing balance into one's life is about escaping the habits of life that we so often trap ourselves in. Some of the lifestyles that many Leaders need to escape include addictions to work and those habits that adversely affect our health and well-being. These lifestyles have impacted a high percentage of Leaders, to one degree or another, over the course of their lives. Lets' take a closer look.

For whatever reasons, many Leaders have developed a compelling desire to succeed and to prove themselves. Often, they are not quite sure who it is that they are trying to prove themselves to, but nevertheless this condition exists. What has helped many to move away from their tendency towards workaholism, is the realization that their lives are not dress rehearsals. This is the real thing! On their death bed, nobody ever says, "I wish I could have spent more time at work."

One strategy that has helped some of my clients escape their addiction to work is to recognize all of the other roles they have in their lives, and the need to allocate specific time to these roles. In addition to their profession, some of their other roles may include spouse and parent. In fact, some of the Leaders I know find it helpful to have a chart on their office wall that reminds them of their other roles that they must play, if they are to experience a balanced life.

Another idea that seems to work well for others to escape workaholism is to shift gears by going to another activity. I know that if many of my clients allow themselves, they could quite easily work late each and every night of the week. There never seems to be a shortage of business related things to do. What works well for many Leaders is to terminate their business day by shifting gears. Whether it is going for a walk, a run, or simply doing some personal errands, this shift allows them to move away from work into other areas.

One of the things that has helped others is to get involved in a non-business recreational activity. If it weren't for a sport or hobby, many Leaders would find it too easy to work non-stop. A sport or hobby, such as golf, fishing or music gets you out of the office into a totally different environment. The benefit that people enjoy from this is that it propels them into a completely different circle of friends. This helps to focus the mind on things other than what is happening at the office. In doing so, it relieves stress and frees the subconscious mind. It is only once the subconscious is allowed this freedom that it is available to produce some of the exciting creative results of which it is truly capable. Another benefit is that the release of stress promotes your physical well-being.

If you are in a Leadership role, let me strongly suggest that you need a hobby or sport to help you escape the ravages of workaholism. Find something that interests you and do it!

In recognition of the fact that they really are their own most valuable asset, many Leaders I know have taken great interest and pride in their own health and wellness. In addition to being very careful about their nutrition, they make it a point to exercise on a regular basis.

The funny thing about exercise is how little you really have to do to experience some wonderful results. I encourage my clients to move their body across land for a minimum of 40 minutes at least every other day. If you are not involved in another active sport, you may decide to exercise on a daily basis. We now realize that we all don't have to be running at world record speeds to benefit from exercise. In fact, one of the best exercises is walking. By getting into walking it really can serve you in two ways. First of all, it can help you shift out of a work mode and secondly, 40 minutes of walking each day is great exercise. Another suggestion that seems to work well is to start each day with a brief 15 minute stretching routine. Many Leaders I know tell me that they feel a lot better and more eager for the day ahead when they tune up their body every morning.

Leaders Are Readers

There is a saying that "the only difference between the person you are now and the person that you are going to be in five years, is the people that you meet and the books that you read." I will leave the people meeting up to you but let me encourage you on the topic of reading. Based on my experience of working with Leaders, I firmly believe that the most successful Leaders are readers. What are they reading? There really is no shortage of excellent books out there. I suggest that you find somebody that you respect and ask them what books they have read lately. Their suggestions could give you some ideas about where to get started.

Reading is a commitment to your own development. It serves to introduce you to new ideas that you may not have experienced otherwise and allows you to think with another person's mind. In doing so you will be stretching your own mind. With all of these benefits, is it any wonder that Leaders are readers.

As a Leader you really are your most valuable asset. By committing to your own preservation and renewal you are assuring yourself that you are living your life to the fullest.

Action Plan ... Converting Ideas Into Action

1. What sort of actions can you take to add a greater sense of balance to your life?

2. If you acted on these ideas, what would be the potential impact?

3. What are you waiting for?

"Visioning without action is merely a dream. Action without vision just passes time. Vision with action can change the world."

Joel Barker

The Language of Success

The use of language is a very powerful Management Tool that properly used will enable you to mobilize the thoughts and actions of others. If information is the basic raw material for creating new knowledge that in turn creates change, what are the primary practices that cultivate and nurture a more effective flow of information?

My experience is that the corporate culture of any organization supports either effective or ineffective communication practices. The latter is deadly as it often traps you in your past, playing a game that no longer exists. The recognition of these inappropriate practices is critical if any organization is to accelerate into the future. Practices create habits and just as there are good and bad practices, there are good and bad habits. So what are the practices that support the healthy habits that will enable your people and your organization to succeed to its full potential of performance, productivity and profitability?

Sharing Background Conversations

Simmering below the surface of many work groups are deeply embedded differences of opinion and interpersonal issues. Examples of this would be strongly held views on the direction of the company or opinions on personal behavior. These issues are seldom spoken or addressed and as a result serve as an anchor that keeps so many people from moving forward. Background conversations, those unspoken words that keep us trapped in the past, are incredibly costly and counterproductive. For me, if there is an issue, I would much rather have it on the table where we can work to understand it and then if possible resolve it and move forward.

Simply put, those background conversations need to be moved into the foreground so that those critical issues of trust, personalities and performance can be confronted and resolved.

Dialogue versus Discussion

Discussions are the language of business. In a discussion, I attempt to influence you in such a way that you see things the same way as I do. Dialogue is something very different. Dialogue is about being open and receptive to other's ideas. It is only once your mind is open and receptive that you are able to actively engage in learning and discovering new ideas. The kind of ideas that will enable you to grow in all aspects of your life.

Discussion is about which viewpoint is right or wrong. Dialogue is about a willingness and receptivity to exploring all of the possibilities and seeking to clearly understand their underlying premises.

Alignment before Agreement

Alignment is "what" we are going to do. Agreement is "how" we are going to do it. Far too often the traditional "control" style managers are quick to seek agreement, the "how" before they have secured a strong commitment to the "what." In the absence of a strong acceptance to the "what" of business, is it any wonder that other members of the team are less than committed to the "how?" And should we be at all surprised when others allow deadlines to slip and miss critical targets? Of course not! The sad reality is that by going for agreement before alignment, many managers consistently set themselves and their people up for failure.

What is Missing?

"Who or what is wrong?" rather than "what is missing?" is another faulty communication style practiced by superiority or control type managers. The problem with this critiquing or policing mindset is that it is all about the past rather than the future. It focuses on the problems rather than the opportunities, the issues and personalities rather than exploring new ideas.

When we ask "what or who is wrong?" we create a culture of fear and it naturally leads to blaming somebody or something. When asking the more powerful question, "what is missing?" we are engaging others to look into the future, consider the possibilities and find a better way.

Escaping the Tyranny of Polarization

I know that for far too long I saw the world in either/or terms. Conditioned as I was, it was just too easy for me to see everything as either open or closed, hot or cold, good or bad, right or wrong, up or down, hard or soft, introverted or extroverted, dependent or independent.

What I have come to realize is that the most successful Leaders see far beyond this limiting mindset of either/or to step up to the wonderful world of possibilities that and/also helps to shape. The apparent contradiction of my limited, highly polarized way of thinking kept me from exploring the possibilities of a more balanced approach. One that often allows us to pursue multiple pathways concurrently. The interesting thing about the intriguing paradoxes of life is that we don't have to resolve them, all we really have to do is manage them.

In her book "When Giants Learn to Dance," Rosabeth Moss Kanter identifies some of the paradoxes Leaders often experience:

1. Think strategically and invest in the future - but keep the numbers up today.
2. Be entrepreneurial and take risks - but don't cost the business anything by failing.
3. Continue to do everything you're currently doing even better - and spend more time communicating with employees, serving on teams, and launching new projects.
4. Know every detail of your business - but delegate more responsibility to others.
5. Become passionately dedicated to "visions" and fanatically committed to carrying them out - but be flexible, responsive, and able to change direction quickly.
6. Speak up, be a leader, set the direction - but be participative, listen well, and cooperate.
7. Throw yourself wholeheartedly into the entrepreneurial game and the long hours it takes - and stay fit.
8. Succeed, succeed, succeed - raise terrific children.

9. Communicate a sense of urgency and push for faster execution, faster results - but take more time to deliberately plan for the future.

10. Decentralize to delegate profit and planning responsibilities to small, autonomous business units. But centralize to capture efficiencies and combine resources in innovative ways.

We need to shift our current position from the tyranny of either/or to the absolute sheer genius of and/also. As with the yin and yang of life, seemingly opposing forces can complement each other. In doing so, it allows us to pursue multiple pathways that will multiply our success.

Together, these five practices can significantly enhance the increased flow of information in your organization. These practices, the frequently repeated actions of yourself and others, can alter the habits and results of your corporate culture.

1. Moving "Background" conversations to the "Foreground" so they can be understood, addressed and resolved in a way that allows us to move into the future.

2. Shifting from "Discussions" to "Dialogue" so that we can move away from a right or wrong perspective and examine all of the possibilities.

3. Seeking "alignment" before shifting to "agreement" and in so doing, securing the real commitment of all of the people.

4. Focusing on "what is missing" as opposed to "who/what is wrong."

5. Utilizing the absolute sheer genius of "and/also" rather than the tyranny of "either/or."

The quality of our conversations will impact the quality of our future. By changing our communication practices, we are taking the first step to transforming how we do business. If we do not make these changes then we are guaranteed one thing and one thing alone. A continuation of the past.

Isn't that the definition of insanity? Doing the same things over and over again yet expecting different results.

If you recognize the fact that your future needs to be something very different than simply a continuation of the past, then you need to take a close look at your communication practices. These communication practices create your corporate culture that will determine your future. By changing the way you communicate, you will be cutting with the past and engaging the hearts and minds of your people in such a way that will produce an inspiring and successful future.

Action Plan...Converting Ideas into Action

1. Of these communication practices shared by successful Leaders, which do you think would help you the most?

2. Why do you think these communication practices hold the most opportunity for you?

3. If you were able to develop these communication practices, what kind of changes would you hope to see?

"The difference between Leaders & dreamers is courage and commitment. The courage to get started and the commitment to keep going."

Ross Buchanan

Practices of Exemplary Leadership

In their book "The Leadership Challenge," the authors Jim Kouzes and Barry Posner report the results of their research into Leadership. What they found is that Leadership is an observable and learnable set of practices. Their findings support my beliefs that for those of you who wish to enhance your Leadership Effectiveness, you can do so through a combination of persistence and desire.

Based on survey responses and in-depth personal interviews, Kouzes and Posner have identified the top five practices demonstrated by exemplary Leaders. They are:

1. Challenging the process
2. Inspiring a shared vision
3. Enabling others to act
4. Modeling the way
5. Encouraging the heart

Let's take a look at each of these practices.

Challenging the Process

It is easy to sit back and maintain a mediocre status quo, but challenge is the opportunity for greatness. In Leadership and Life, it isn't "what is" that matters as much as "what could be."

Leaders, real Leaders, seek out and accept challenging opportunities to test themselves and their teams and search for creative strategies to improve their organizations. With everything else around us changing, it is only natural that people do their best when they are given the opportunity to change the way things are. Inspiring others to reach and stretch beyond their previous limits is a vital quality of Leadership.

And where does the best advice for creativity and innovation come from? Not exclusively from the Leader. No, the best ideas for change in a healthy corporate culture come from everyone. Gone are the days when the innovative ideas are the exclusive realm of a handful of senior executives. To be successful today, what is called for is a wealth of Leaders. Leaders in every area, and at every level continually contributing creative and innovative ideas.

Successful Leaders challenge the process by getting outside of the box, playing to win and listening to their people and their customers.

Inspiring a Shared Vision

Visions are like the Leaders magnetic North, they give direction and purpose to all of the people. If plans are logical, then visions are emotional and are designed to help their people dream about how good it really could be. Visions, properly implemented, can engage the minds and hearts of the people with a powerful passion.

But for a leader to have a Vision is not good enough. It needs to be shared with and accepted by others so that it can become the powerful force it is capable of becoming. A Leader's role is to envision an uplifting future and then to enlist and engage the hearts and minds of others in the passionate pursuit of this vision.

Far too often I discover early on into a corporate assignment that there is no vision. In the absence of a vision, the focus is on the past rather than the future and problems rather than opportunities. The sad news is the kind of rot and resistance that can take over in the absence of an inspiring shared vision. The good news is that the positive impact of a shared vision can accelerate a business from mediocre and stagnant to successful and progressive in short order.

Enabling Others to Act

As a Leader, your success is no longer dependent on you, yourself. As a Leader we must succeed as our people succeed, through the combined will and competencies of others. To achieve exciting results in business today, people must be working interdependently. Attracting the right people, sharing your expectations with them, and then getting out of their way is a major challenge for any Leader who has been conditioned in the traditional command and control model of management. The successful Leaders of today recognize and act on the need to trust others.

In trusting others, those who may have traditionally seen themselves as followers step up to accept their role as Leaders, recognizing the need for a wealth of Leaders at all levels and in all areas of the organization.

By promoting cooperation, building trust, and sharing information, Leaders help all of their people to become empowered and to contribute to the success of the organization in a significant and meaningful way.

Model the Way

My experience has been that most Leaders have developed a philosophy on how the organization should run, as well as a set of values about employees, suppliers and customers. Successful Leaders recognize the need to "walk the talk," to maintain consistency between their words and deeds, and to serve as a model, an example for everyone.

It is through this process that trust and credibility is built. The kind of trust and credibility that Leaders require to help their people achieve all that they are capable of.

Encouraging the Heart

Success in business does not come easy. Getting all of your people to work together to succeed is hard work and cannot be accomplished without connecting with both the mind and the heart of all involved.

Leaders have high expectations of themselves and others. They know that they need to provide all of their people with direction, encouragement, personal attention and feedback. Leaders make people feel like winners and winners like to continue to raise the bar.

In order to truly encourage the heart, successful Leaders focus on recognizing the individual's contributions to the success of the business and celebrating the accomplishments of the team on a regular basis.

Together, the Five Practices of Exemplary Leaders demonstrate to us that Leadership is not about extraordinary, charismatic actions of a handful of elite executives.

True Leadership, the kind of Leadership that is required today, is all about seemingly ordinary people who care enough to accomplish extraordinary things. In the end, Leadership is about personal growth. It is about knowing yourself and believing that you are capable of making a difference, and then learning what you need to know in order to make it happen.

Action Plan....Converting Ideas into Actions

1. How do you think others would score you on each of the five practices of exemplary Leaders? On a scale of 0 (low) to 10 (high), assign a score for each of the practices.

2. Which Practice do you think provides you with the most room for improvement?

3. If you were able to improve in this area what might be the impact?

4. What are some things that you could start doing now to improve in this area?

Credibility!
You either have it or you don't.

In addition to their work on Exemplary Leadership, Kouzes' and Posner's research also examined the Characteristics of Admired Leaders. Over 20,000 people on four continents were asked to select from a set of 224 different values, traits and characteristics. The overwhelming results showed that the majority of us admire and willingly follow Leaders who are:

Honest

Forward Looking

Inspiring

Competent

As a Leader, credibility is vital. The First Law of Leadership is that if we don't believe in the messenger (no credibility), we won't believe in the message. Each and every Leader I know has come to acknowledge this basic principle.

It is interesting to note that the top four factors that contribute to the credibility of a Leader in busines also include three of the characteristics of what media experts call “source credibility.” In analyzing the credibility of any source whether it be a newscaster, physician, politician or salesperson, we typically evaluate based on three criteria:

1. Their perceived trustworthiness
2. Their dynamics
3. Their expertise

Notice how similar these three criteria are to honest, inspiring and competent - three of the four factors that determine credibility in a Leader.

We need to believe in our Leaders. We need to believe that their word can be trusted, that they will do what they say, that they are enthusiastic about the opportunity and that they have the knowledge and skill to lead.

In business and in life, you either have credibility or you don’t.

Action Plan...Converting Ideas into Actions

1. On a scale of 0 to 10, how do you think your people would rate you for each of the four primary factors that contribute to your credibility?

2. For the factor where you felt others would score you the lowest, what sort of things could you do to improve this score?

3. If you were able to enhance your credibility, what sort of changes would you expect to see?

"It must be remembered that there is nothing more difficult to plan, more doubtful of success, nor more dangerous to manage than the creation of a new system. For the initiator has the enmity of all who would profit by the preservation of the old institution and merely lukewarm defenders in those who would gain by the new one."

Machiavelli

The Discovery Mindset

If there is one thing that I can guarantee you, it is that life is a process of change. Our degree of sanity amongst the chaos created by change is not determined by the curves that life throws at us but rather how we respond to the changes of life. The good news is that there definitely is a way to maintain serenity, sanity and balance.

One of the factors that I see shared by successful Leaders is what I call a Discovery mindset. This is very different than the traditional Safety mindset practiced by traditional managers. The Safety mindset essentially says, "Life is stable, predictable for the most part, and to a high degree something that I can control." If you see life as the above sentence describes, then you secure your sense of well-being from knowing that life will unravel as predicted. This way of thinking is called the Safety mindset and is primarily practiced by those who are focused on just making a living. The Safety mindset focuses on trying to desperately cling to the past and seeks order and stability in a world where they just don't exist anymore. In fact, even if order and stability were possible, they probably would be the last thing you should be seeking as they could very well serve as anchors that will trap you in the past as your competition races by.

On the other hand, there is another mindset that says, "Life is complex and constantly changing and I enjoy discovering what works best at any given time, in any given situation." If you see life as this scenario then you are open and receptive to seeing life through the eyes of others and will achieve your sense of well being from constantly learning and growing. This way of thinking is called the Discovery mindset and is primarily focused on living in your environment rather than attempting to control your environment.

Now, it is very likely that all of us have a bit of both a Safety and Discovery mindset in our mental makeup. Having said that, the tendency is to want to control life rather than live life.

One of the things that I have learned from the hundreds of Leaders that I have had an opportunity to work with is that the most successful Leaders, the ones who consistently rise to the top in the chaos of a constantly changing environment, are those who have learned to live life using a Discovery mindset.

The Safety mindset just does not allow us to function effectively in a world in which change at times seems out of control. The Discovery mindset embraces the paradoxes, complexities, contradictions and uncertainties of life and enables us to feel in charge of ourselves even when everything else around us appears to be going crazy.

For me personally, I can tell you that abandoning the Safety mindset and learning to apply the Discovery mindset has been a big breakthrough. I realize that it is okay for me to not know what to do next or to admit that I just don't know all the answers. Heck, I don't even know all of the questions! But I do know that with the Discovery mindset, I can learn to grow and work in alignment with my current reality rather than fighting all of the forces of life and trying to control something that is clearly uncontrollable.

At the heart of the Safety mindset lies a desire to "play not to lose." Fear of losing leads to setting very low expectations to ensure that these expectations are met. On the other hand, the Discovery mindset is about "playing to win." It is about stretching and reaching, always knowing that there is a better way.

Some of the key differences between the two mindsets look like this:

Safety Mindset	Discovery Mindset
• Fights with change	• Embraces change
• Clings to the past	• Reaches for the future
• Attempts to control others	• Trusts others and wants to learn from them
• Polarizes life as "either / or"	• Seeks balance and recognizes the absolute genius of "and / also"
• Independent	• Interdependent

The Discovery mindset is not something new but it is something that is called for among Leaders now more so than ever before. The paradox of it all is that in today's world stability really comes from letting go of the compelling need for safety and instead, reaching out to grab the future that you can flow in alignment with. The kind of future that a Discovery mindset enables you to live.

"The jungle fighter symbolizes where the corporation has been; the virtuoso of interpersonal skills is the corporate future."

Shoshana Zuboff
Harvard Business School

EQ

We are in the early stages of what I believe to be the next revolution in Leadership. Recent and rapid developments have now brought the concept of EQ - Emotional Quotient to the forefront of many business discussions.

In the past, our likelihood of success in life has been based on IQ - Intelligence Quotient. Research now validates what many of us have known for sometime. Now, more and more Leaders are recognizing the value of EQ to complement IQ. It is important to note that this is not an either/or thing. Success will come to those who cultivate and balance both IQ and EQ.

Emotional Intelligence is best described as the ability to work creatively and cooperatively with others. Think of this! Two firms competing in the same industry, located across the street from each other. Both companies employ a hundred talented, technically rich professionals with an average IQ of 140 each. Collectively, each company has a total IQ of 14,000. Which firm will succeed to the greatest degree?

The answer has to be the firm with the highest collective EQ. By working together in a cooperative and collaborative way, we can't help but to leverage and multiply our overall success.

In the rapidly changing competitive world of today, we need to optimize the combination of both IQ and EQ, especially when it comes to teams and trusting others to respond and react to fast-breaking opportunities. What price do we pay for low EQ and an over-dependence on IQ? Consider for a moment the adverse effect that low EQ can have on areas such as Decision Making, Leadership, Communication, Teamwork, Customer Loyalty and Creativity. If we develop a corporate culture in which IQ exclusively rules the day, it is only because the Leadership Team allows it to happen. When the Leadership allows IQ to rule, we chose a bad and inappropriate master. Again it is not IQ or EQ but rather the balance of both. If we have erred in the past, it has been to place too much emphasis on IQ and not nearly enough importance on EQ. But like a lot of things in life, this view is changing rapidly.

You will be interested to know that a study of 3,000 successful professionals identified twenty-one characteristics they shared in common. Of the twenty-one shared characteristics only two, Mathematical Reasoning and Language Skills, were related to IQ.

Nineteen of the twenty-one characteristics of successful professionals were about EQ not IQ. Emotional Quotient not Intellectual Quotient. The heart not the head.

Some of the critical factors that I see contributing the most to EQ would include self awareness, control, persistence, resilience, zeal, compassion, self motivation, empathy and a social deftness. Together, these factors combine in a way that enables people to flourish both in their intimate relationships, as well as in their professional lives. These factors form the basis of character, self-discipline, altruism and compassion. The price we pay in an absence of EQ is absolutely scary in terms of misguided and terrifying childhoods, hateful marriages, poor physical health and ruined careers.

But there is good news! EQ can be learned. The life skills that contribute to the success of people who excel in life are all acquired traits. If you want what others have in terms of an enhanced EQ, it is never to late to start.

"Absolutely everything in your organization rises and falls based on the Leadership Effectiveness of your key people. Yes, absolutely everything!"

Ross Buchanan

"No Excuses" Leadership

Open Book Management is a progressive concept that could have significant impact on the profitability of your business. Personally, I prefer to think of this new way of running your business as "No Excuses" Leadership, but we are really talking about the same thing.

"No Excuses" Leadership is about shifting profit and loss responsibility out of the the hands of a few people and into the hands of everyone in the organization.

The most powerful and immediate impact of such a strategy is that you help your people shift their focus from their task to their job. Most employees are confused about the difference between task and job. In fact, they typically think their task is their job. Wrong! Employees' tasks vary from receptionist, to shipper-receiver, to salesperson, to accounts payable clerk to purchaser and vice president. Make no mistake about it, the people in all of these tasks share the same job. That job is to help their organization make money. Once people start to see the difference and understand that the creation of profit is everyone's responsibility, exciting things start to happen.

Why "No Excuses"? In the absence of meaningful financial information, and with people focused on "tasks" rather than jobs, it is easy for most people to pull out the old "that's not my job" in order to escape responsibility or accountability. And, they are right. In 99% of North American businesses today, profit and loss are not the employee's job. But it should be, and the good news is it can be. In an organization that shares all of its pertinent financial information with the employees, making a profit becomes everyone's business!

One of the keys to the successful implementation of a "No Excuses" Leadership Plan is simplicity. The more complex and sophisticated the plan, the less likely the opportunity for success.

The four key components of a successful plan include:

1. Providing all of the people in the organization with as much of the financial information that you can, in as timely a manner possible.
2. Helping everyone to understand your financial information and the impact it has on the profitability of your business.
3. Immediately cease and desist from any further annual pay raises. All increased compensation in the future must link to the enhanced fortune of the company.
4. Get out of their way! You have hired the best people to do a job and given them the corporate resources and financial information to do it. Now let them do exactly that!

Sure, it will not be easy. You will run into a variety of icy patches on the road to "No Excuses" Leadership but let me assure you that the journey will be fun and the destination will be profitable for all of the participants.

In my experience as a Leadership Adviser, I am constantly amazed by the number of organizations that are run as if they are in never-never land. The never-never land of revenue with only a few of the players focused on the critical issue of profitability.

As an example, a salesperson driven by and reviewed on revenue stays at $100 per night hotels, eats $40 meals and will travel to another city to meet one or two customers. A salesperson who is profit-driven, reviewed based on his customers' contributions to profits, and whose colleagues are aware of his traveling expenses, will stay at $75 per night hotels, eat $20 meals and make certain that he meets with as many customers as possible while he is in the area.

The more I think about Open Book Management or "No Excuses" Leadership, the more I realize that what we are really talking about is treating employees like the mature, capable adults they really are. There is no doubt that this concept of new thinking requires radical shifts in how we do business. But in the words of Yogi Berra, "If you do what you always do, you will get what you always got." There must be a better way, and more and more progressive businesses are starting to realize that "No Excuses" Leadership can be the better way.

"The new reality of the great game of business calls for more Leaders actively coaching their people and less managers keeping score."

Ross Buchanan

Coaching For Commitment

Over the course of the last few years as I have worked with Leadership Teams, I have come to realize that Coaching in the business arena may very well be the most under developed and underutilized talent available to any manager. Think about it! How many times have you been coached in your business career. Far too often the answer is "never."

Yet we know from a wealth of other experiences in life, the kind of immediate, significant, positive impact coaching can have on an individual's performance. Companies don't succeed - people do! And the people who achieve the most significant results are those that are fortunate enough to benefit from on-the-job coaching. The kind of coaching that can move unsatisfactory performance to satisfactory, or even better, helps people to step up from satisfactory performance to superior.

In my mind, the Traditional Management Model looks something like this:

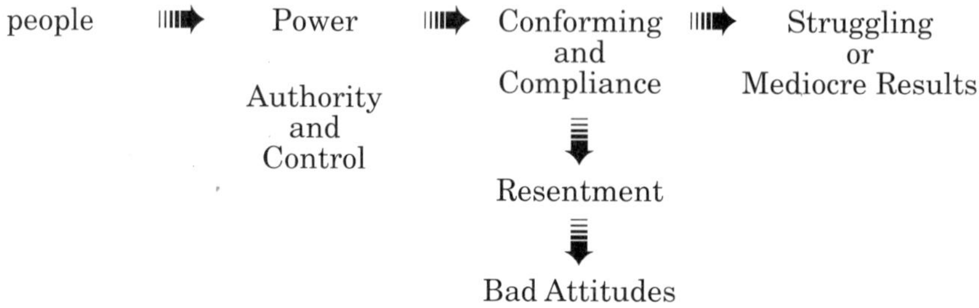

In the past, this model based on Power, Authority and Control has been good enough. But let me suggest to you that in today's world, the best you are going to achieve with a control mindset is short term, struggling or mediocre results. In a world of accelerated, global competition, if you as a manager are prepared to accept satisfactory performance, then you must inevitability take responsibility for a loss in competitiveness, a dramatic decline in your share of the market, stagnant capital growth, and worst of all, decreasing profitability.

People who work "under" the Traditional Management Model as illustrated do conform and comply to doing mediocre work because they have to. What is needed is an enlightened Leadership Model that will encourage people to do superior work because they want to.

When you take a look at the Traditional Management Model, which is practiced by the majority of North American businesses, you will see that it starts with a small p for people. Quite frankly, traditional managers simply do not place the value on their people that they are truly deserving of. Ironically, in this environment, over a period of time, the really good people are often enticed away to more appreciative employers and sometimes all that is left is truly small p people. In the absence of principles, passion and pro-activity, all you are really left with is a warm body and not much else.

In the Traditional Management Model, managers govern based on the power, authority and control their position gives them. Perhaps this is enough to capture the backs and hands of the people but certainly not enough to excite the minds and hearts of people in the way that any organization needs to really excel today.

This misuse and abuse of power, authority and control then leads to the employee conforming or complying to the request. Buried just below the surface of this compliance is often a rotting resentment. A resentment of his or her job, the employer, the manager and themselves for allowing this situation to develop and continue. Eventually resentments resurface and are often manifested in a bad attitude.

What impact can a bad attitude have on an individual's performance? Now multiply your answer to this question times the number of bad attitudes that the Traditional Management Model is capable of spawning. You can very quickly determine the magnitude of the damage. The fallout from this inappropriate approach to management can leave your company looking like a nuclear test zone.

And what about the results? At best struggling, mediocre and very short term. People, good people, the kind of people you need to attract and develop if you are to succeed, just will not put up with it anymore.

Now consider the possibilities for an Enlightened Leadership Model that looks like this:

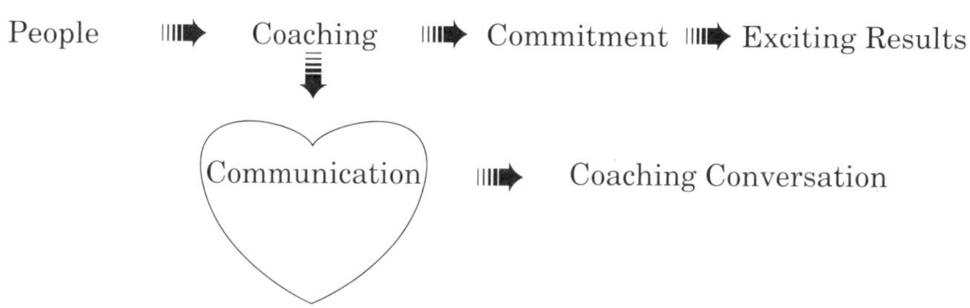

Like the previous Traditional Management Model the Enlightened Leadership Model starts with people. You will notice that people is with a capital P. One that truly reflects the value of all of the individuals who cumulatively contribute to your ongoing success.

Rather than relying on power and authority, the enlightened Leader engages in a Coaching role. The kind of Coaching that enables him or her to connect with their people in different ways and coach them to greater levels of productivity and performance.

You will see that at the heart of Coaching lies Communication. Your most valuable Coaching Tool is the Coaching Conversation. My experience is that the number one reason managers fail to Coach their people is simple. They don't know how. It is for this reason that I have designed and developed a model for Coaching. One that has proven its worth for my clients in extensive real-life field testing. You will find more about this powerful Coaching Tool later but let's move on for now.

A critical component to the Enlightened Leadership Model and Coaching is the kind of commitment that it is capable of igniting in the hearts of your people. So what is commitment? Well, I don't know about you but I see commitment as the key to superior performance and productivity. Webster's Dictionary defines commitment as "dedication to a long term course of action; engagement; involvement." I know from my own empirical research that committed people share two specific behaviors:

1. Committed people are very focused.
2. Committed people are ready and willing to make personal sacrifices to help their organization or team achieve their goals.

Elsewhere in this book, I have dedicated an entire chapter to Focus so I will not be repetitive here other than to encourage you to help your people identify their own priorities. No one can climb an entire range of mountains at once. We can only do it one mountain at a time. Often, in the absence of a clear corporate Vision and with fuzzy feedback from those they report to, people are simply confused about what their priorities should be. Guaranteed, by sitting down with your people to help them develop a crystal clear picture of what their professional priorities are, you will help them define their bull's eye and get back on target.

The other characteristic I see shared among committed people is the willingness to make personal sacrifices. And in this day and age, who is going to make personal sacrifices unless all of the other pieces of the Leadership puzzle are in place? Inclusion, Appreciation and Accountability link the employee to the true impact of their performance on the corporate vision.

I think that a lot of what we are talking about when we discuss personal sacrifice is really about the connection to long term sustainable achievement rather than short term, immediate pleasure. Often, we must make sacrifices today for a greater tomorrow. It is only committed employees who are willing to demonstrate a high degree of personal sacrifice and my experience is that commitment is best cultivated through "eyeball-to- eyeball" coaching.

The Productivity Ladder

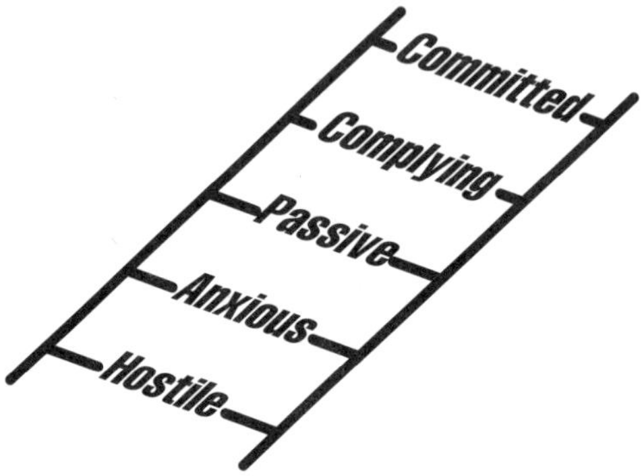

When you examine the Productivity Ladder, you quickly realize that there really is not any reasonable option other than "committed." In today's competitive world, if your people are not committed you are in big trouble! None of the other options even warrant a second consideration.

Results? What can I say. Seldom does a day go by that I don't receive at least one call from a client talking about the kind of exciting results that they have been able to help their people achieve through Coaching. When it comes to Coaching in business, there really isn't any room for comment on the scorecard. It simply delivers. No other single Leadership skill has the potential for producing powerful and immediate improved results in the areas of performance and productivity the way that Coaching does.

As Managers, we are responsible for producing results. No matter what kind of results you are responsible for, you need to achieve them through other people. As we see in the Traditional Management Model, a mindset of power, authority and control may be able to produce satisfactory, short term results through policies, rules and punishment, but that is the very best that they will ever achieve. I don't know many managers who think that an average or satisfactory level of performance is good enough today. What is called for in this world of ever accelerating global competition is Leadership and Coaching that taps into the discretionary power and potential that each individual possesses. The discretionary power that allows people to achieve the kind of superior results that they want to.

"Good enough" just is not good enough any more! If you and your people are stuck at satisfactory, you better look out because my prediction is that your competition is going to be racing past you. What we need to be shooting for is a superior level of performance. Superior performances are achieved because the employees, the holders of that discretionary power and potential, have chosen to contribute their discretionary reservoirs to achieve superior levels of performance. So the question then becomes, "How do we, as managers, tap into that discretionary reservoir of power and potential that links directly to performance and productivity?" The answer, I believe, is a simple one. Simple and not the least bit surprising. The answer is Coaching!

Combined with some of the other more progressive Leadership philosophies such as Open Book Management and Self-Directed Work Teams, Coaching for Commitment cannot only complement all of the good things you are already doing, but in fact, leverage each of your improvement initiatives in such a way that it will multiply your overall success - the success of all your programs, the success of all your people, and the success of your organization.

Unfortunately, the sad reality is that in many businesses today, everyone runs for cover when there has been a sighting of the boss headed in their direction. Typically, they know that one of two things are about to happen. They are going to be told what a terrible job they are doing or they are going to be loaded down with yet another task with an unreasonable deadline.

Sometimes they will be surprised. Rather than the expected "dressing down" or "loading up," what they will experience is a manager paying them a brief and insincere visit asking about how things are going and then rushing off to something more important.

People want to connect with people. It is the personal touch that really matters. We want to connect with our managers who show that they really do care about us and our contributions.

Coaching is the process that will enable you as a manager to connect with your people more often. It is about staying in touch and in tune with your people and all of the things that are happening around you. Guaranteed, all of the "walking around" in the world will not help managers enhance the performance and productivity of their people until they stop walking and start coaching. The key here is eyeball-to-eyeball coaching conversations that will allow you to work with your people to clarify goals, set priorities, and agree on standards of performance. In addition, a Coaching Conversation is an ideal time to celebrate the successes, show appreciation, reinforce the vision, and to learn first hand from the employee.

The Coaching Conversation

As I have worked with clients to help them enhance their effectiveness as Leaders and Coaches, I have come to realize that the best Coaching Conversations share seven key characteristics:

1. They are one-to-one.
2. They are performance related.
3. They are timely.

4. They are specific.
5. They are managed.
6. They achieve or maintain a positive work relationship.
7. They focus on the future.

It is important to note that the kind of coaching in business that we are talking about be carried out for the most part in a one-to-one environment. Of course there are times for team coaching, but for the kind of individual performance enhancing results we are looking for a one-to-one scenario is best.

The second characteristic of an effective Coaching Conversation is that it needs to be focused on performance related issues. Examples of performance related topics would be the inability of the employee to achieve production levels or the employee's habit of not being on time for meetings.

Coaching Conversations need to be timely with often the best time being "now," but again, watch out for exceptions. If heated emotions prevail maybe later would be better. The important part here is that the time to have a Coaching Conversation is as close to the specific unsatisfactory performance as possible and not six months from now when you sit down for the annual Performance Review.

The fourth characteristic of an effective Coaching Conversation is that it be specific. One trap that many managers fall into when attempting to coach their people is their inability to speak in specifics. Generalities are not good enough. To tell someone that they are "always late for meetings" has little credibility in the eyes of the employee because surely they can remember at least once when they were on time for a meeting. We need to be specific. "The reason I wanted to talk to you is that you were late for Monday's 9:00 a.m. meeting. You kept all six of us waiting for 15 minutes and I wanted to talk about what we can do to ensure that it doesn't continue to be a problem in the future."

Without a doubt, the most effective Coaching Conversations are managed. Managed by whom? By you, of course. Now don't get managing and dominating confused. In fact, as you will see, a good 90% of the time in an effective Coaching Conversation should be spent listening.

To properly manage a Coaching Conversation, we need to plan. What do we hope to achieve? What are we going to say? What kind of response might we expect? What are all of the possibilities?

The sixth characteristic of a successful Coaching Conversation is that it allows you to achieve or maintain a positive work relationship with the employee. Be careful here. We are talking about a positive working relationship not a strong social friendship. There really is a difference, isn't there?

Focus on the Future, the seventh characteristic of a successful Coaching Conversation, is equally important. We need to be talking not about the past, as much as we need to talk about the future. Focus on the Future!

So there you have it, seven key characteristics of the most successful Coaching Conversations. The kind of Coaching Conversations that can help you increase the performance and productivity of your people and the profitability of your company.

The CUS Model

1) Confronting 2) Understanding 3) Strategizing

Once we come to realize that Coaching just is not optional for successful managers and it must become a core Leadership competency, the next question is how? Without a doubt, the most effective Leaders actively engage in Coaching. The good news for those who have neither the competence nor the confidence in Coaching in a business setting is that we can learn the principles, skills and strategies that research shows the most successful Leaders utilize to coach their people to enhanced levels of performance and productivity.

The CUS Model has been designed specifically to help you learn a process that can become a powerful performance-enhancing strategy for an effective Leader. If you think there is a touch of irony in the name of the CUS Model, you are right. You will see that the CUS Model is at the opposite end of the spectrum from what you would expect to hear when you "cuss" somebody out. Yes, the irony is intended and it does make it easier to remember the CUS Model, doesn't it?

CUS Model

Confronting, Understanding and Strategizing
...a Pathway for Improved Performance

Step 1 - Confront

Limit Their Resistance. Be Specific: Give a clear and concise statement of the issue.
Focus on the Performance Issue. Limit the statement to single issue.
Look to the Future. Express desire for change, don't request a reason for failure.

Step 2 - Understand

Reduce Resistance. Have a free flowing conversation. Drop the agenda. Focus on the individual's concerns, not your own.
Gather Information. The Master Communications Skill of Life ... Seek first to understand, then to be understood.
Agree on Issue. Secure mutual understanding of issue & causes.

Step 3 - Strategize

Establish Ownership of Issue. Create solutions and agree on follow-up.
Maintain Relationship. Review. Reinforce solutions and ownership.
Commitment. Be Positive. Comment on potential positive impact of solution and individual's contribution.

As you can see, the CUS Model is a step-by-step process that enables you to work with your people in such a way that will help you coach them to greater levels of success.

The key here is to stop intellectualizing the Coaching Conversation and start actualizing it. Once you have reviewed and contemplated all of the steps to the model, I would suggest that you work with a colleague to role-play some possible scenarios and then provide each other with open and honest feedback. It is only once you have had an opportunity to play with the model that you will then have the competence and confidence to put it to the test of reality.

In workshops, we invest time practicing the CUS Model. Guess what? The practice works! Leaders realize how ineffective they have been at holding their people accountable for their performance and how powerful a coaching tool the CUS Model really is. Once people start to get the hang of it, they become increasingly excited. Excited about the kind of potential that the CUS Model has for capturing the discretionary power and potential of their people and helping them step up to the next level of performance.

As you role-play the CUS Model, here are a few things you would want to keep in mind:

1. Remember the wise words of Ben Franklin, "People are best convinced by reasons that they themselves discover." Coaching is not about telling but about helping your people come to their own realizations.

2. Coaching is about "letting go," not controlling. "If you give a man a fish, you feed him for a day. If you teach him how to fish, you feed him and his family for an entire lifetime." Sure, it is easy to jump in, take control, and make it happen now. But are we searching for what is easy or what is most effective? One approach produces short term results. The other is about investing in a successful future.

3. If during the Coaching Conversation, you are talking more than 20% of the time, you would want to give

your head a shake and ask yourself what is happening. Control of a Coaching Conversation does not come from talking. If all you are doing is talking, then you are dominating the conversation. True control for the Coaching Conversation comes from asking questions and listening. Leaders are Listeners.

4. Patience, Patience, Patience. Remember, we want to hear what the employee thinks should be done. We need to give them a moment or two to reflect on the situation and the solution before we demand a response. If we really want to open people up, we need to be certain that our communication style is not shutting them down.

5. Reread the Advanced Communication Skills for Leaders chapter with special emphasis on Listening and specifically, the Third Party Conversation. The key is to clearly understand the magnitude and depth of that third conversation.

My intent here regarding the Coaching Conversation and the CUS Model is not to duplicate the work that is more effectively done in the participatory environment of a workshop but to alert you to the possibilities and show you a proven model. A model that has helped other Leaders increase their Coaching Competencies and in turn, help their people enhance their levels of performance.

As managers, our success is dependent on the combined wills and competencies of others. I don't know about you, but seldom have I found a business tool that has the potential for positively impacting others the way that the Coaching Conversation and the CUS Model do.

Action Plan...Converting Ideas Into Action

1. If you were to take a more active role in really coaching your people, who might be a good person to start with?

2. What performance related issue would you want to address?

3. Ideally, what could be the best result you could aim for?

4. If you could help this person move in the right direction on this issue, what could be the impact on the employee, the rest of your team, and yourself?

5. When would be a good time to schedule this Coaching Conversation?

"The significant problems we face today cannot be solved at the same level of thinking we were at when we created them."

Albert Einstein

The Eleven Laws Of Effective Leadership

Based on my experience of working with successful Leaders across North America I have developed "The Eleven Laws of Leadership". These are laws that have worked for others to help them enhance their "Leadership Effectiveness". What kind of impact could they have on your success?

1. If you are not including your people you are excluding them, and in doing so, eliminating the possibility of securing their commitment.

2. If your people do not feel appreciated they are feeling taken for granted. How do you feel when you are taken for granted?

3. People want to be held accountable for their performance. If they are not being held accountable then the message is clear. Nobody cares! And if nobody cares why should they?

4. The mother of all Leadership errors is that Leaders

think the purpose of their people is to serve them rather than the other way around.

5. Your mavericks will bring you your future. Give them room.

6. Abandon the "control thing" and set your people free to achieve the kinds of exciting results that they truly are capable of .

7. Listening may very well be the most effective Leadership skill. "If you are talking all you are doing is repeating something that you already know. If you are listening you might learn something new."

8. Leadership success without successors is not success at all.

9. Leadership is about channeling your scattered resources into one powerful beam of energy. Focus, Focus, Focus!

10. The ultimate Leadership mindset — Inter-dependence. The language of "we" rather than the language of "me".

11. There can be no more powerful engine driving an organization to success than it's vision of the future.

Conclusion

Can we all be great Leaders? Probably not. But I am convinced that we all possess the capability to become better Leaders. The concepts that I have shared with you have helped others develop their "Leadership Effectiveness". Is there any reason that they can't do the same for you?

The key to your development as a Leader is "You!" You possess all of the potential that you require to become the best that you can be. If you are serious about unleashing your Leadership talent, now is the time to take action to find the effective Leader within yourself. The investment you make in developing your most valuable asset, yourself, will pay you dividends the rest of your life.

In Leadership, like anything else in life, you really are the steward of your own destiny.

We Can Help!

People everywhere are clamoring for change in the way business is done. The "old ways" of doing things are simply not cutting it anymore. The traditional management approach has become a prescription for failure. The world has become too unpredictable, too volatile, and too fast moving for such an uninspired approach. The new realities of business today call for enlightened, effective Leadership. Without it, your organization is almost guaranteed to take a beating.

In order to chart a successful course into the future, you need to enhance the critical Leadership strategies of the key people in your organization. Strategic Training's highly effective *Leadership Strategies Workshops* are designed to help you do just that.

Everyone is talking about the need for better Leadership. We seem to be drowning in an ocean of books and articles, all promising simple formulas that will transform us into powerful Leaders. You know it is not that simple! Anyone who has tried to be a Leader knows the results are not so spectacular or predictable.

Leadership Strategies is unique. It will be unlike any program you have ever experienced. A proven approach to acquiring the skills and strategies necessary to develop as a Leader. That is because *Leadership Strategies* is not just an event. This Professional Development Program is not an end in itself but rather a new beginning. The beginning of a renewed commitment to addressing the critical issues of Leadership in your organization, and enhancing the "Leadership Effectiveness" of your key people.

There is no doubt about it! The future belongs to those Leaders who recognize the opportunity, and commit to optimizing and maximizing their Leadership talent. People who are "managed" do their jobs because they "have" to. A Leader inspires people to do their jobs because they "want" to. The ability to lead people can be developed.

I hope you enjoyed reading this book as much as I enjoyed writing it. If you are interested in knowing more about our Leadership & Coaching Development Workshops or our unique and inspiring Keynote Presentation *Licensed to Lead,* you are invited to contact me personally at 604-684-7888.

Ross Buchanan

Strategic Training International
#700 - 555 West Hastings Street
Vancouver, BC, Canada V6B 4N5
E-mail: ross@stigroup.com
Phone (604) 684-7888